No Finer Way to Die

A true story of living with

death and dying

Plus Encouragement for Caregivers

by Kathleen Adcock Haskett

Voices in Print Publisher

Nashville, TN USA

This book is written in grateful memory of
Elizabeth "Betty" Buckman Adcock Bowers
- November 7, 1917 to September 6, 2003 -

No Finer Way to Die; A true story
of living with death and dying

Text and illustrations by Kathleen A. Haskett, unless
  otherwise noted

Copyright c2005 by Kathleen Adcock Haskett
Paperback Original ISBN 0-9771963-0-5

Voices in Print Publisher
P.O. Box 210249
Nashville, TN 37221
website: www.voicespublisher.com
email information: info@voicespublisher.com

Library of Congress PCN 2005931891

Publisher's suggested cataloging
Haskett, Kathleen Adcock, 1946-
No Finer Way to Die; A true story of living with death
 and dying / Kathleen A. Haskett
Includes bibliographic references and index
ISBN 0-9771963-0-5 (pbk.)
1. Death - 2. Grief - Psychology 3. Inspiration - Spiritual 4.
Caregiving - I. Title

foreword

To the mother, sister, sibling, daughter, father, son, dear friends -- who have allowed me the great honor of walking softly beside your gentle love and courage, and who have found my presence supportive -- please know that however I may continue to be of support to you will continue to be an honor.

My thoughts and prayers trace trails of tears -- it was you who knew your loved one better. Perhaps, through you, I too will come to know the strength and courage you once knew, and now so deeply mourn. Loss cuts a deep and rutted groove through which to pull the fragile wheel of life, we all must turn. My deepest respect for your living and for the grief you've borne.

kAh

Table of Contents

Introduction

I love telling the story of my mother's profoundly sweet death, no doubt extra sweet to me, due to the inverse experience of my father's death. More than one extreme loss in my young-adult life created the early necessity of learning to walk with grief. The mix here, of personal story and professional information, comes from two different parts of my brain -- the part of being a daughter, and the part of being a licensed counselor. These parts have become good friends, but it wasn't always that way.

Before I could receive the blessing of Mom's death, I had to build a new receiving place inside of me. I learned that I needed a new receiver when I learned that mine was not operating properly. I learned my receiver wasn't operating properly when I failed two marriages. I learned that I failed at marriage because I wasn't healthy.

I learned that I wasn't healthy when I learned what a healthy adult is. I became ready to learn about being healthy when I was so tired. I learned I was so tired because I had a malfunction in my brain, caused by incorrect thinking. I learned my incorrect thinking was an attempt to adapt to terrible pain. I learned the name of my pain was grief.

While grief wasn't new to me, I had no idea about the connection to grief and my lack of having a healthy receiving place inside. For readers newly experiencing grief, I am hoping this book will provide some short cuts in your learning curve.

I knew my father had died long before I was ready for him to die. I did not know that my attempt to avoid grieving his loss had shut down my receiving place for any healthy intimacy. At the time of his death, the drawbridge on my heart shut quickly, but not before the trauma of my father's death poured terrible pain, like poison, into my heart. Steel arrows appeared. They came to keep out anyone who would hurt me again. Surviving alone seemed to be superior to the risk of being hurt by loving someone again -- at first.

This is my story that outlines the years of crawling on my knees, as the proverbial woman seeking bread crumbs from beneath the Master's table. At least sitting now, I offer it to you in the form of a small, but rich meal.

I wasn't certain if I was ready for Mom's death, so I was more than a little surprised to know how profoundly blessed I would feel by the process of her dying. My history of painful deaths and losses had led me to have a long, unanswered list of questions beginning with, "Why?" Finally, I believe I have begun to understand a few of the answers. This writing reflects my compassion for those of you experiencing the terrible agony connected to "Why me, Lord?" "Why now?"

Experiencing losses gives us the right to ask, but the asking doesn't necessarily mean we have a receiving place for the answer. This book is written to help you to find where you are on the journey of having a receiving place for the abundance of living, especially if it has been locked, as mine was. For those whose receiving place was never wounded or closed, you may find this easy reading. Read as quickly as you want. Wounded hearts, on the other hand, may benefit from both slow reading and re-reading.

My hope for you (and for me) is joy, honor, and dignity of dying as peacefully and wonderfully as my mother died. *No Finer Way to Die* is my contribution to you, and to the memory of my mother. I have tried to eliminate offensive levels of preaching, teaching, and poor writing. Mother wouldn't like those parts either.

Sadly, I cannot eliminate my deep concern about the prevailing violence in our country, and daily losses that reflect immaturity, drug and alcohol abuse, greed, rigid thinking, arrogance and ignorance on a national scale.

I am especially concerned for my generation of baby boomers, and the beautiful generation of our adult children (mostly in their thirties), bound for taking care of us in our old age. Short of an intentional change of direction, the clash that is currently minimized with our children's generation will undoubtedly sprawl into the lives of our beloved grandchildren. I see many baby boomers engaged in avoiding their pain from losses, using such *coping strategies* as shopping, eating, drinking, abusing prescribed medications, neglecting their feelings, and procrastinating about their aging. This does not provide a healthy model for the generations following us.

I know (because I've lived it) that awareness and processing of losses results in increased intimacy and healthy relationships, so that when death does visit, the way is easier for everyone involved. This idea for a wiser and more mature community to walk into the final phase of life, was *greatly* influenced by my mother's gracious living before she died in 2003. The title for this book was inspired by Mom's final nurse who said:

"Surely there is no finer way to die; this is the way I want to go."

This book is meant to encourage the infusion of dignity and respect into the years of growing older, empowering while simplifying living, so that you may die with tranquility, if you have anything to say about it. How would you rather die? What is the road that will lead to this standard?

Historically, we have set some of our strongest models for living based upon lies about materialism, finances, and accumulation of wealth being equal to the ultimate success and power. We have made icons of famous people, when the real value of life is in enduring and responsible relationships to each other and our planet. There is always time to change, I hope, despite substantial dedication to wrong formulas.

I am grateful to my father for twenty years of strong and generously loving parenting, despite the abrupt ending of his life, and to my mother who took up the baton and carried it well for thirty-five more years. I am hoping the truth I claim in this book will resonate with your own stories, enough to invite you into a larger, and mutually shared truth.

In her spiritual book, *The Rock that is Higher: Story as Truth,* Madeleine L'Engle writes that stories, fiction or not, may represent truth. As a counselor, much of my advice flows from the story of my reconciliation with the pain of life.

I find myself writing this as a love letter to you, or as if sitting together, talking in and around these topics, the way friendly children pass in and out of a jumping rope. I believe the topics, not the style, are difficult, and, as in conversation, we would dip intimately into our truths, and then back off to gain perspective. These breathing spaces also would allow us to accept differences in each other's views.

I can only write of my story that has both the lightness and darkness from which I eventually derived my vision of the shapes of things as I see them. What else is there, aside from faithfully waiting past the shadows of the dusk and dawn for clear sunlight or directional starlight? Maybe we won't really see the light until we die!

In other words, this is my experience, my story, my vision, thus far. I cannot remove *all* of the wandering multiplicity of my thinking, for reasons both of inability and defiance. I hope the counselor part brings sound advice, building blocks of facts, analysis, and practical suggestions. I hope the daughter in me brings my personal insight and emotion that supplies the mortar for these building blocks. My prayer is that both you and I are blessed by God in this sharing.

I don't talk too much about my fear of death in this book. My generation, as children, practiced for the event of a nuclear attack-- some of us by hiding under our desks. Of course, we didn't think or speak of the real and inevitable losses if such an attack were to have occurred, (and what desk would provide protection!) In itself, this history has a fear and trauma base, which I do address in this book.

I was actually unaware of how much I feared my own death until I looked into my surprise at the general public's fearful response to 9/11. I had to ponder, "Why am I *not* experiencing the same fears they are?" As I explain more later, I had mostly locked up my horror related to death at the time my father was killed.

Conveniently (for my fear), I moved twenty-some times in my adult years, so my fear of being known by others didn't surface until I truly settled into a community.

Subconsciously, I had isolated in order to stay hidden from being killed. It still feels pretty risky to mention my full name on the front cover. I see now, my isolation was a form of *self-sabotaging*. This well-intentioned fear resulted in holding me back instead of protecting me. (Chapter 4: *The Glitch, p. 35* regards this thinking that results in self-sabotaging.) I spent more than thirty of my adult years subconsciously rationalizing, "If I stay hidden, I will not be murdered like my father."

This book is my effort to be true to myself and my life-long desire to write, made easier now by a deep desire to share my grateful memory of Mother. Part I summarizes my story of living with deaths and multiple losses.

I consider the sum of living includes: receiving, losing, grieving, recovering, surviving, living and thriving -- hopefully before we die. Furthermore, the difference in the order of these is more than an existential rhetoric, and sometimes life's simple addition is replaced with uncharacteristic algorithms.

The sum of Care Giving and Care Receiving can turn the dance of losses and gains into a slow-motion movie, with frightening repetitions and aberrations. The vast opportunities and challenges of caregiving fall beyond the scope of this book. I feel qualified only to respect and encourage those who enter such holy domain -- thus, Part II.

I found some of the resources for caregivers (books, organizations, seminars, etc.) to be amazing. Take hope and assistance from those who are truly available to help and nurture you through this difficult transition. I admire the courage and the profound gifts in *both* the care giving and the care receiving. Beginning resources, and questions to ask to help you find the right caregivers can be found in Part II.

My invitation herein is to:
- Learn the characteristics of grief.
- Learn tools for grieving painful losses.
- Seek the definition of healthy.
- Increase your experiences of safe, vulnerable intimacy.
- Know when you need professional help.
- Learn what to share with the professional(s) on your team.
- Consider more fully the holiness of dying peacefully.
- Learn how to prepare for the death of a loved one.
- Personally, be less fearful of death.
- Know that you are enough.
- Remember Betty.

This seems a tall order for a small book. I hope I have created manageable bites for those in pain. If you are currently in fresh grief, I invite you to glance over the Table of Contents and go immediately to any title that beckons you. Wherever you are on your practical learning curve will launch the truth of your emotion and insight into your current losses. Moving toward your fuller truth happens as you access your internal blueprint for healing. Accessing your blueprint is the difficult part I have tried to address. Once you find it, healing is natural. As much as something in you needs to heal; something inside of you longs to do the healing. The result of healing is healthy, peaceful living.

From a divine moment in my own healthy (enough) place of living, I received and witnessed the blessing of Mother's peace-filled dying.

Thank you friends of Betty's who believed in me and sent me notes of encouragement to continue my writing. To Mozelle Core, thank you for grounding me about editing.

Thank you, Max, for your daily strength and support. Thank you, my children, for walking our dreams hand-in-hand, and sharing in growth. Thank you, readers, for being my witnesses.

Kathleen Adcock Haskett

To order more books, please send $12.00 plus $4.00 shipping and handling to:

Voices in Print Publisher
P.O. Box 210249
Nashville, TN, 37221

Other products and insights may be found on the Voices in Print Publisher's web site, www.voicespublisher.com -- as it unfolds in the future.

Orientation to this book

For guidance about how to grieve, see *Loss and Grief*, and *Grief Work*. To prepare for a forthcoming loss, consider the exercises found in the *Appendices*. To open up conversations with an aging loved one, read *Preparation, Family* and *Wellness*. If you struggle with compulsions or addictions, read and re-read *The Glitch*. If someone you know is dying soon, you might read the Chapters, *Spirit*, and *Mind and Body*. Consider reading the subtopics of "Regrets and Confessions," "Permission," "Consequences," and "Timing" -- **with them.** To feel less lonely, share your story with someone who will *safely* listen. When you need a break, read *Gratitude* and *I Am Enough*.

Appendices provide hands-on opportunities. Copy them, and work through the questions with a small study group. Share your truths.

In the event that you are early in the process of caring for an aging loved one, go to the references in Part II, and then back up to learning about grief, for it will surely accompany you on your journey.

Reading, an integral part of my upbringing, continues to guide me. Therefore, I have supplied a partial reading list. Books about life and grieving can be like Saturday night buffets; take only what you need for the time, and come back as often as you like. If you find a favorite author, search for their other works. Finally, be patient with your place on the learning curve; you are enough for today.

ONE

No Escape

For years I felt forced to grieve behind closed doors. I greeted life angrily and contentiously, feeling as if one hand was tied behind my back. Not incidentally, my father died with both hands tied behind his back.

My journey with grief has led me through the extremes, and a situation in-between, that I call grief purgatory. Learning to make my everyday existence as normal as possible does not change the fact that at least one loss was horrid, another was chronic, and most recently (the death of my mother) a memory of sweetness and blessing. All were landmark experiences, spread over more than three decades. Furthermore, the horrific death of my father happened just blocks away from where my mother died so peacefully, thirty-five years and twelve hours later.

I think of grief purgatory as a grief-in-limbo, a term I learned from Active Parenting, (headquartered in Georgia.) This is the grief mothers of permanently disabled children experience. It is the grief that spouses, parents and siblings experience when a beloved family member is suffering a chronic illness, or living a lifetime in prison. This grief does not naturally resolve itself, but remains constantly slippery underfoot as it hosts unfolding losses over time.

Most situations with death fall somewhere along these continuums...slowly to suddenly; tenderly to violently; thoughtfully to impulsively; sweetly to angrily; ready to unready; wisely or not; with or without love -- and everywhere along each continuum of death -- **loss is the evidence**.

Grief, the interpreter of losses, cuts a deep groove in our brain's gray matter. Grief filters the experience of loss through family beliefs, individual temperment, historic events, and cultural sanctions and taboos, making it difficult to identify grieving as an emotion separate from what other people think, say, believe, and expect of us. It also hurts.

The scope of this book cannot begin to cover the influence of such historic watersheds as the Crusades, the plague, the Holocaust, World Wars, and genocide, to name only a few, that have left indelible imprints on mankind's beliefs related to death and grieving. Neither can this book edify any cultural customs, strange or otherwise, regarding rituals around death and dying. If you want such a clever book, I suggest reading *Death* A User's Guide* by Tom Hickman, available in Delta Paperback, wherein sanctions and taboos are extensively explored.

Long-standing traditions form the mountain range, over which many theorists have poked their heads. Their efforts to produce meaningful interpretations have bulged the disciplines of religion and theology, philosophy, science, psychology and mysticism. Humorists will never stop taking a whack at death. Everyone is affected, and sooner or later, everyone has to settle somewhere on a ladder, a climbing rope, or simply out on a limb of their own choosing.

Answers are not easily forthcoming for individuals who struggle beyond the norms. Those with pathology, or with mental disability, or mental illnesses do not escape the issues of grief, but may sadly live outside a community who grasps the fullness of their needs.

Four parameters of grief can be listed. They are:

1. the severity of emotional responses,
2. the level of readiness to heal,
3. the length of mourning, and
4. the eventual resurgence of feeling alive.

Unfortunately, they are too individualized among those in grief to report on them in a general way with any accuracy. Don't let anyone tell you that you "should only grieve" a certain number of months or years, for example. The only accuracy I can share on these will be my own truth about my own experience. It will exactly match no other.

It is my experience that the emotion of grief will often trump all other emotions; it will have its day and its say. Your need to grieve will undoubtedly outlast your interest in doing so. Grief is a mighty test of endurance.

I have also found grieving, while seldom an enjoyable process, an essential activity to becoming healthy and feeling whole again. These two major traits of grief (its capacity to trump and its necessity to heal) underscore both my story, and the instructional component of this book.

My Experience: Grief seemed impossible to manage, or to make go away, until I learned to walk with it hand in hand, as with a big gray buddy. I believe grief will torture even the best of persons until the presence of grief is acknowledged and understood. Even then, the

sensation is one of having tamed a tiger into an unruly kitty. Getting to know grief is a little like befriending a wild thing.

Living as we do, on a planet populated by some who speed through life with reckless or helpless abandonment, we can expect to learn sooner, rather than later, about *the Grim Reaper, the Last Roundup, Eternal Night, our Passing,* the *End,* or *Termination* -- to name just a few common phrases, not altogether euphemistic, for death.

Loss as Death

Why don't we call death death? Are you fearful to ask, "Is she dying?" Or, "Are you dying?" After all, we are all dying, some sooner than others. None of us knows our exact time of departure. Maybe staying ignorant seems best to you, both of the process, and all the ramifications of death, rather than being reminded of this time of guessing about our own or someone else's mortality.

The time of the final departure, however, should not be confused with the much needed preparation for living wisely and lovingly into the final phase of life with a loved one. Such is a time of dying that may span more than a few years. Denial and delusion abound around the concepts of a loved one dying.

A Myth: The human seed, when fertilized, grows, taking approximately nine months to become a full term baby. If the baby lives; if the baby has no defects or character flaws; if the baby has a loving family; if the baby is born into a home with enough income; if the baby is taught only loving lessons; if the baby is nurtured physically, emotionally, and spiritually; if the baby grows up in a cultural environment free of dysfunction, rich with appropriate challenges, and fully supported in an absence of pain and loss; and if the baby grows into a well-educated child, both healthy and happy, then this person has not and may never experience the pain of loss or death. (Oh yeh?) **End of myth**. Even in the "perfect" physical world, there would be changes and losses in the living and evolving of that world. The circumstance of being human is one of constant change.

What four year old hasn't experienced a real or sense of a death, either of a grandparent, an ideal or of a deferred desire? However, most four year olds will not have the language for their losses. Nevertheless, they demonstrate moods, temperments, and unusual sadness at times.

How many ten years olds have experienced the death of their parent's marriage? How many twelve year olds, the loss of their favorite pet? How many fourteen year olds have had to move away from their best friend? Or their best friend mysteriously stopped being their best friend? How many seventeen year olds have lost their innocence? How many nineteen year olds have lost their first loves, or been fired from their first jobs?

This book explains how recognizing and accepting loss and death as an everyday experience can lead to the creation of strong and intimately caring relationships within the *same* environment as the losses.

Perhaps you believe that in your lifetime you have mostly escaped death and loss. This could be true, or you might be in denial. The deeper, more impassioned life you live, the more you stand to lose. If you have loved more than most, then the greater the challenge will become in your life to live with the losses that will occur, or have already occurred.

In high school, I loved to sing. I had heard that I had one of the best solo soprano voices in school, and so I believed I did. I also had the personality to pull off the dramatic role of Nellie Forbush in the high school's production of South Pacific. High school politics among the teachers cut me altogether out of the triple-cast lead, and my own great disappointment resulted in my taking myself out of the play. I didn't know how to handle the loss of my idealism and innocence. It was a powerful lesson in life's math, that two plus two may not always equal four. This incident would be entered on a time line as one of my earliest losses.

Creating a Loss Time Line

Seeing the extent of your losses is the first step toward accepting them. The tool to help you do this is called a **Loss Time Line**, and is explained in Appendix A (page 176).

This tool will help you to summarize the losses you have experienced and the age at which you experienced them. The age is important because we are developmental in our natures.

For example, a five year old who loses a parent will learn to cope (with some help, I hope) with this death. This same five year old, as he reaches new developmental stages, will renegotiate his loss, based on his expanded understanding, new experiences, and increased maturing. In other words, he has to grieve again at ages 8, 10, 12 15, 17, and every time he gains a more developed perception of life. (Most people don't realize this characteristic of grieving, and wonder instead why they don't "get over it.")

Not surprisingly, this same person will also deal with the loss of his parent when he has a child of his own, and of course when that child turns five. Developmental stages continue throughout adulthood, although they are farther apart in the adult years.

Creating a time line of losses provides a visual of your loss experience that will help you to begin breaking the denial our society has (in most cases) urged you to maintain around death and losses and your need to grieve. Appendix A: **Loss Time Line** (page 176) provides questions for developing important insights into your own losses. Recognizing your losses, and healing from them, will strengthen your abilities to nurture yourself and others.

There are many misconceptions about the nature of grief. "If I begin grieving, I won't quit" is inaccurate. The next chapter covers why bygones cannot be expected to simply go away, even if you have declared them history.

TWO

Loss and Grief

Losses create a ripple effect, the way a stone tossed into a quiet pond leaves noticeable rings in the water for some time after the stone itself has disappeared. The rings seem to extend, one after another, as far as they can go. Ripples off a devastating loss can have a far reaching effect in our life times. We need the truth.

Can we leave bygones alone? If so, how? If not, what do we do instead?

Leaving bygones alone doesn't work well because grief has an accumulative effect. This accumulation of grief complicates the processing of new losses as they happen. If you are currently experiencing or anxiously expecting new loss, you may not have the energy to do the emotional work required to remember and process your previous losses. Resolving your historic losses is more a preventive measure regarding grief's accumulative effect.

It is important to understand that the accumulative effect of the grief experience can make old losses feel as if they are happening again.

This effect can be a powerful distraction from the

needs of the present moment. When the old loss has not been resolved enough, the new grief sticks (much the way Velcro works) to the old grief. This may cause you to feel as if the old loss is re-occurring, or that this new loss is an overwhelming loss, even when it might not be. More than likely, your grief is "adding up."

For example, let's suppose our big gray buddy comes into the doctor's office, and sits on your head. For no apparent reason you begin to cry hard or to feel very angry about your son's sprained knee. Is it really that he's going to miss the end of the basketball season? He's hurt, but he's eleven, resilient, and otherwise healthy. You wonder about your strongly emotional reaction. Not withstanding sports enthusiasm, the presence of accumulated grief can be easily misinterpreted.

You may have discounted the recent change in jobs, the fight you had with your neighbor, and your pastor moving to another church, all within the past several weeks. Grief from these unprocessed losses is now sticking to the fresh grief for your son's loss.

By the very nature of our internal blueprints for healing, losses that have gone ungrieved will come up for a second (or third or more) opportunity to resolve -- especially around the time of new losses. In a way this is handy; we can all use some internal housekeeping. It can also feel invasive, overwhelming, and inopportune.

Our defense systems are burdened and we feel awkward and vulnerable, or doubly so, when another loss happens. When your emotions are "all over the place," it is time to take stock of your need to grieve.

If grief's accumulative factor is left unattended, avoidance systems are often created. I summarize some of these strategies of avoidance with the following headings:

Who's Sorry Now?

No Sadness Here.

Party Time. Drug and Alcohol Use or Abuse.

Spend-Spend-Spend.

Pain is Illegal; Don't Feel.

The Blues.

Hating This Life.

Out Of Control.

Holier than Thou.

Self-Righteousness.

Everyone Else is to Blame/

This is All My Fault.

Angryland

Entitlement.

Emotions, as if on an elevator going between these strategies, often surprises the grieving person with random stops at different "floors".

The result is usually misery, feeling terribly alone, depressed, or as if things will never be better. Attitudes, including: "Men are all shmucks; women are too demanding; I don't like being around children; I hate everybody; Nobody likes me; I'm not the marrying kind" may indicate an avoidance of intimacy because of the painful grief associated with former, partially caring relationships or relationships that were supposed to be supportive and caring, but were not.

Advice to "just get over it, get on with your life, shouldn't you be over this by now?" might all be indicators of a log jam in someone's grief capacity -- often, unfortunately, in the advisor, as much as in the advisee. Either or both may need professional help, or at least a neutral party to support them through their grief work (See the chapter on *Grief Work,* page 48*).*

Complicated grief

It is good to know about this accumulation factor before a parent becomes ill and begins the dying process, but that's not always possible. Sometimes losses happen close together, creating a situation not unlike a nightmare. Compounded losses result in **complicated grief.** Simply put, this grief is difficult to mourn because it is so overwhelming.

The grieving process can also become complicated if unprocessed losses already exist. The loss of a best friend, who died of breast cancer; a miscarriage from a few years back; a secret abortion in college, or the ideal of marriage ever since the realization hit that it wasn't going to happen the way you dreamed, can all complicate the grieving process even years later, if left unaddressed. While each person's content varies, the accumulation of pain is evidenced, especially if you feel you are emotionally grinding to a halt, or at best, moving at a snail's pace inside a shell of existence.

Unresolved grief becomes ever more burdensome with each new loss, which negatively affects our ability to trust and to find hope. The acceptance and serenity so needed around death and dying, find sustenance in trust and hope. Trust and hope, always flowing, move in and out of available choice.

At times, it can be a difficult swim upstream to go against popular opinion and strong avoidance systems in your friends and relatives, to do the grieving you need to do -- let alone when you need to do it. Intuitively most people realize they need to grieve, but they are afraid to seek help, or to ask for time off, or to insist on some quiet time to themselves. Unresolved grief will not just stay in a trunk in the attic forever.

If you do not find time for your grieving, it will often make side trips out of you, through such things as anger, sarcasm, bitterness, rudeness, and inappropriate behaviors. You may even notice too late the hole it has burned in one of your vital organs. Learning to grieve is a necessity, not a luxury.

Secondary Grief

Secondary grief ripples off primary losses. Suppose your spouse doesn't get that promotion you were both counting on, so the move to another state is out, and buying a larger home with a chance to start over won't happen now. These are called secondary losses. Or say the promotion does come through. You are going to move, and you have to leave your best friend. She says it won't matter; you'll be best pals forever. Then she gets married. You're happy for her, but your relationship is feeling the ripples of the changes, and it's not only a new feeling, but you are struck extra hard when she forgets your birthday.

"That's just life," I hear you saying.

True. Acknowledged as such or not, we live with different kinds of deaths everyday. Sometimes it's a water balloon in our faces, and other times it's more like being run over by a semi-truck.

Second-Choice Grief

Consider the pros and cons list you made recently about an important decision. Both pros and cons existed, but you finally made a decision that felt "more correct." Then within hours, or maybe minutes, you experienced the loss of the second choice that, as a direct result of your decision, you will now never experience.

Surprised to know of this? Maybe you call it second guessing yourself, or having qualms, or doubts. I am grateful to my husband who taught me the concept of second-choice grief. It has made my life easier to know that after I have made an empowered decision, the tiger will walk through the house. I simply yawn, sit at the top of the stairs and watch the tiger leave quietly through the backdoor I've left open.

"Goodbye, second choice," I may call out. "Goodbye, other good thing, other possibility, option number two. I will miss you, but I have made my decision."

Then I close the door and take a nap.

Since learning to grieve openly, a freedom resides in me. The capacity to grieve is a helpful skill that has freed me to accept life with open arms. This acceptance and preparedness for death in my life brought me the skills and joy of pulling my beloved dying mother into my arms, and the peace of mind to open my arms and let her go, when the time came that it was right to do so.

Whether it is a child to kindergarten or off to college, a spouse to divorce, or a loved one to eternity -- we will repeatedly need the tools for grieving. There is no escape from the experience of loss, and **while loss is inevitable,**
-- grieving remains our choice.

In Summary: There is no escaping loss and death, which your grief will interpret. You will experience grief over losses both similarly and differently from the ways that others grieve. If left unresolved, grief will accumulate. Grief sticks to itself. Second-choice grief will invite you into doubting yourself and your first-choice decision, even when your first choice was likely accurate. Unresolved grief over losses may be affecting your life now, which can affect your ability to trust and hope. Trust and hope are basic to feeling peaceful about the death of someone you love. Grief will come with losses. Whether or not to resolve the grief will become your choice.

THREE

A Wrong Assumption

I believe there is a misconception that a person in grief "gets over it." Instead, I think we learn to flow with it.

Imagine our thoughts lined up like dominoes, collapsing one on top of the other, because the first assumption (domino) topples in error. Mostly, our brains do not seem that well organized, but the idea of a wrong assumption (or more than one) is worth considering, especially if that wrong assumption is negatively affecting your life and your interactions with others.

IF we don't really "get over" grief, and IF grief that has been left unresolved will stick to the grief of new losses we continue to experience, and IF grief is experienced by people as young as four years old, and regularly throughout our lives, THEN what is happening to all the accumulated grief that people *think* they are "getting over"?

The belief that anyone can avoid, get over, escape, or outsmart the painful part of living is supported by strategies that **do work temporarily.** This has the effect of reinforcing stop-gap measures. Unfortunately, these coping strategies, if left in place over time, exact a terrible cost. Perhaps it is time to question some of the prices we may be paying when we do not learn to flow peacefully between the pain and joy of living.

Stop-gap Measures

1. _Inadequately dealing with life's pain can result in blockages to the mind, body and soul._ Unless something changes, over half of this nation's current population will die from a heart-related illness. How might blocked and congested hearts be related to the attempts to block out grief in your life?

2. _The constant distractions required to take your focus off the pain of losses results in splitting your focus into two or more, less-centered ones._ An alarming increase in numbers of children are being diagnosed with Attention Deficit Hyperactive Disorder, and/or a pediatric form of Bipolar Illness. In addition to the possible effects of preservatives, additives, caffeine, and the polarizing effect of computer games, I wonder if a parent's inability to teach his child to grieve has anything to do with this increase? What losses for children are directly connected to the absence of routine living situations? What connection might a child's focus have to do with parents who cannot ever seem to agree?

3. _Because grief from continued losses is accumulative, eventually its unprocessed presence hangs like a dull weight in the mind._ Without a clear distinction between depression and grief, popular ways of avoiding grief may contribute to misdiagnosis, and the high volume (more than 90 million people) taking anti-depressant prescribed medications. In addition alcohol and illegal drugs, used in an effort to numb the pain of losses, contribute greatly to the mismanagement of this pain. Practicing strategies that avoid pain for long periods of time, eventually obscure the original causes of pain, making resolutions even harder to find. Pain that is both obscure and unresolved may be in danger of presenting itself as anger, helplessness, lonliness, unhappiness or numerous physical ailments that are difficult to diagnose for root causes.

4.   Grief is about memory and remembering. Avoiding grieving may coincide with avoidance of memories of traumatic or unpleasant losses and correlate with avoidance of relationships that could build new, happier memories. Not wanting to remember losses can result in not remembering the positive things either. Furthermore, Alzheimers and diseases accompanied by dementia may be exacerbated by unresolved grief and loss.

5. Isolation results from the unavailability to grieve in communion and contributes to a level of lonely unhappiness that can literally affect the body's chemistry. Something as major as a hurricane or a tsunami is at least temporarily mourned openly by many, and results in encouraging, helpful community support.

On the other hand, the losses of a job, a partner, a dream, or a heart's desire represent more personal losses that are held closer to the chest (the heart?) and are often approached alone. While it is admirable to work through your own problems sometimes, the chemical changes that may go unnoticed can create larger problems than the original loss.

The chemistry ping pong inside the body begins

to shift appetites, moods, interests, and actions. Over and under eating, for example, may bring on weight issues. Cognitive distortions about body image and mood swings contribute to eating disorders. Substance abuse and abuse of prescribed medications can create chemical downward spirals. Further isolation and potential addiction can result from computer misuse and overuse in areas of games, shopping, and pornography that may bankrupt both finances and relationships. When these coping strategies are used for long periods of time, the chemical pathways "back to normal" are even more difficult to rediscover.

Coping with losses often follows familiar and common themes. Familiarity makes them seem acceptable, unless you begin to notice their connection with problems (such as depression, disease, abuse, addiction, arguments, family strife, and divorce) that interfere both with peaceful and prosperous living. The glitch, as I call it, undergirds most of the common and (not always subtle) coping strategies.

FOUR

The Glitch

The glitch in this case is in our society's mental software. Generally, it has to do with inaccurate mental math that affects all of our living activities, including how we approach death and dying.

The glitch begins with thinking simple substitutions will replace grieving the difficult and complicated losses we experience.

In most cases the substitute and the loss are not even related, but a pleasant response to the substitute makes us "feel better," we think, about the loss. A mental gear slips and associates the two in our minds. We pursue the doing and achieving of things that simultaneously abandon our need to address our pain. The pursuit (of quick-fix-to-feel-better-now activities) travels in the opposite direction from healing.

If you find yourself exhausted, out-of-control, feeling regret, shame, embarrassment and/or overwhelming sadness, it is wise to search for what is the true cause of these. Instead, our society instructs you to find a quick fix. Out of habit, you try to find something to keep you busy or make you feel temporarily better. Anything to keep you from considering sad, lonely, or overwhelming feelings. Watch T.V., spend some money, go to a movie, get online, eat, smoke, drink something. Go ahead, it will fill in some lonely space, but it won't "get rid of" grief. It won't take the place of doing grief work, if that is what is truly needed.

The experience of substituting too much of something for too little of something else is the glitch in the experience of glitch thinking. The mental math doesn't work.

About the Chemistry

Your thoughts affect your chemistry. Every organ's function and every function's by-product can be described in terms of chemistry. Moods and feelings can chemically swing the hormones and neurotransmitters (that can also swing back). Each day's energy level directly reflects an internal chemical balance of which we may or may not be partially aware. An extensive discussion on the chemical science in our brains, and how that relates to love, has been well written by three psychiatrists, Thomas Lewis, M.D., Fari Amini, M.D., and Richard Lannon, M.D. Their book is entitled *A General Theory of Love* (Random House, New York, 2000 - Vintage Edition, 2001).

I believe it is important to mention our chemistry since the process of arriving at a peace-filled death has much to do with healthy chemistry. Simply stated, food fuels and creates the chemistry we burn, absorb, and store, and helps us generate every kind of activity our minds and bodies do. Healthy chemistry of the air we breathe and the water we drink is essential for healthy cells that form a basis for healthy organs. While you may prefer a more poetic view of the human body, the chemical view has a kind of accuracy.

Since the glitch is about mental math, this discussion of chemistry focuses on two parts of the brain that correspond with very different sets of thoughts and behaviors.

The *Reptilian* brain, located at the top of the spine at the brain stem, is called such because it is considered the oldest part of our brain. A more evolved part of our brain, located more centrally is referred to as the *Limbic* brain. Understanding the differences between these two parts of who we are is significant to finding serenity. Lewis, Amini, and Lannon discuss this at length, but for our sake, I will offer a mere skeleton of what happens.

The reptilian brain's functions are related to basic survival. We instinctively react from this part of our brains, to fight, flight or freeze in order to preserve ourselves. The drive to procreate our species also derives from the reptilian brain. The mechanism that urges procreation fuels sexual activities that create a chemical pleasure known as an orgasm. The reptilian brain ignites over both experiences of fear of danger and sexual pleasure. Chemically, I refer to this ignition as the *high of the brain*. These physiological highs relate to such habits as television watching, food (and alcohol and caffeine) consumption, profuse spending, and repeated, high-risk sexual activities, to name a few. Because the high of the brain is short-lived, it must be repeated often to maintain a sense of achieving the high.

Initially, the emotional experience related to this kind of high is one of pleasure. However, the pleasure has a limited, and usually short duration. Food and substance addictions are habits of attaining a chemical brain high that doesn't last long, so the demand repeats itself. Tolerance to the chemical change is developed and a progression toward accelerated demand occurs.

The limbic brain, located more centrally, houses the activities that relate to compassion, nurturing, and non-sexual intimate relationships. For this reason, I refer to the igniting of this area as the *high of the heart*. Yes, I know it is still *inside* the brain, but the high of the compassionate nature is far more evolved than the reptilian part of who we are, and I believe it correlates to the distinctions often made between the "heart" and our more base nature.

The kind of chemical high that is relevent to a peaceful death of a loved one comes from the high of the heart (of the brain). Born from feelings of a joy-filled soul, there are no words to adequately describe an orgasm of the heart. Major tranquility comes the closest.

The high of the heart does not numb the emotions. It is not the result of hype about activities and achievements that dodges our deeper passion for living. Those who live for accomplishment will experience a progressively demanding need for another high of the brain. Substitutions of less toxic habits (habits good for you) wane in comparison to the instantly pleasurable habit of reptilian brain highs. It is this reason addictions are so difficult to overcome. The internal chemical math moves into repeated errors, as healthy and well-being falls out-of-reach for anyone caught in this trap of seeking brain orgasms from the repeated uses of addictive, and chemical habits. What sounds like something that should be great for us (repeated pleasures) turns into something that eventually destroys us.

When scientists were learning about this part of the brain, they had pigeons hooked to electrodes that stimulated this pleasure seeking part of their brain each time they pressed a bar with their beaks. A similar bar, not connected to pleasure, but rather to the provision of their food was ignored for the repetitious action of stimulation to their pleasure centers. They literally starved themselves to death, seeking the brain high. Even with much larger brains, and more choices, we humans have been known to do the same thing!

Those who live for being (rather than for doing) are more likely to exerience the high of the heart. In order to experience the peace and joy of the death experience, the do-ers have to focus more on being than doing.

A Convoluted Paradox

When one seldom experiences the high of the heart, our biology works to fill the void. In the process of trying to fix painful feelings, the biology and society's training inevitably make things worse. The survival brain kicks into a higher gear to fill a void it cannot fill. This is what we see on the surface: Not feeling loved? Watch more T.V. Not feeling loved? Drink more alcohol. Not feeling loved? Eat a pound cake. Not feeling loved? Buy something.

The math won't change, however. The formula of doing something too much because something **else** is happening too little, is wrong. Too much of something for not enough of something else is the glitch in our software that is currently affecting us as a nation.

The general corporate focus is blatantly advertising (from the Internet to T.V. commercials) by sexualizing the sale of products, romanticising lust in movies, and acting out violent actions that are meant to excite the neural pathways and reactions of the reptilian brain. These appear to be efforts to match our base desires and reactions to the use of their product through association. For example, they attempt to associate a car with personal strength, status, and power, or a name brand with being hip or popular. All of these promotions are meant to connect to the <u>feeling</u> of the best preservation of oneself.

Unfortunately, few people understand their individual chemistry, let alone the interaction between our natural responses and our reactions to the mercenary greed of those trying to sell a product. Are you aware of the compelling chemical responses inside of you to the commercials geared toward incensing the high of your brain? Imbalance is difficult to avoid when it is constructed from both outside and inside our circumstances.

Additional things complicate our chemistry, as if we needed more! Food additives and preservatives affect our chemistry balance negatively. Fast foods and empty caloric foods work at several levels to create imbalances. We not only receive compromised nutritional value from these foods, but the stress of eating quickly, on the run or while we drive, creates another layer of chemicals the body will attempt to counterbalance. Thirdly, and probably less noticed than the first two, is that non-sexual, nurturing and intimate connection is missing. Fast and stressful meals eliminate the sense of communion (taking bread) with others. Our distracted desires to fill ourselves often keep us from even noticing that we are not creating the kind of intimate, caring connection that will sustain us through the worst of times -- that time of losing someone we love, to death. Ironically, poor chemistry within "loving" efforts may bring us closer to dying.

What about Fear?

What do our bodies do with fear? I address fear in nearly every chapter as part of the whole problem, rather than addressing it as a problem standing alone.

Briefly, fear is yet another stimulant to the reptilian brain, demanding it to find calm, or at least "control" quickly. Temporary fixes come to the rescue. They look like this: I fear being alone; I'll watch more T.V. I fear being alone; I'll drink more alcohol. I fear being alone; I'll take a pill. (By now, you probably get it.)

Studying chemistry may help your awareness, but it probably won't slow down the list of people adding more chemicals daily to our air, food, water, beverages, clothes softeners, cleaners, fabrics, paints, personal care products, all to give us a so-called improved quality of life.

Remember how great the sheets smelled when they came in from hanging on the clothes line? I have never found a synthetic fragrance to compare to that childhood memory. This thought was to give you an opportunity to feel a shift in your brain. There is no fear (for me anyway) associated with the great smell of sheets dried in the sunshine on the plains of Colorado. I remember this and nostalgia flows from my Limbic brain. It is quieter there -- no fear.

Feeling fear is a choice, unless you are traumatized. Regard fear -- see Appendix B: Living with Less Worry and Fear (page 178) -- and continue to learn how to resolve your losses as you learn how to balance those parts of your brain that have very different agendas.

The Search for Balance

While science is able to trace some of these chemical pathways, the difference between "'heart and head" can be remarkably connected to different chemical responses in these two locations in the brain -- the reptilian brain and the limbic brain.

The reptilian brain responds with quick, briefly satisfying kinds of chemical climaxes to those things it perceives necessary to its survival. It is not analytic, but rather reactionary. It creates habits to preserve itself.

The limbic brain responds with compassion and nurture, creating long-lasting, "heartfelt" kinds of relationships. A climax from this part of ones brain is a discovery of joy and peace, encouraged by understanding. The experience of being loved instills patterns in the limbic brain. We draw from our limbic brain the understanding, loving, and cherishing of others for long-lasting relationships. Striving for a balance of these (self-preservation and loving connection) requires knowledge, discipline, and healthy choices.

When I tell people that my mother's beautiful death was life altering to me, I usually receive one of two different responses. Either they understand, because they have experienced a similar high of the heart, or they look at me as if I'm crazy because they have no such experience. They cannot comprehend death that is a blessing. We live in a culture that has become ever more distanced from the high of the heart, and therefore, the levels of acceptance of death.

The relationship built inside the heart of the (limbic) brain has a chemistry that will flow with grief, talk with a dying loved one with compassion, fearlessly walk the path with them to their exit, and ultimately have the beauty of this memory to empower them the rest of their lives.

On the other hand, the more prevelant high (that of the reptilian brain) will distract us from finding this deeper passion. Fueled by our pain and fears, our reptilian brain creates roadblocks to the quieter path to serenity. Traumatic loss manifests in one such roadblock. An important reason to learn to grieve is to open the way for a high of the heart. Ignorance of the effects of trauma and painful losses may create the void into which we pour all our energy to accomplish something, only to feel empty after accomplishing it. In a society preoccupied with profits, the reptilian brain responses have become sought after, and exalted.

The first words I hear about Christmas, in early Fall usually have to do with the economic forecast. The concern is how big the sales this year will be, compared to the previous year's sales. I, for one, am asking, "What can we do to make this year's holiday season more meaningful, not just more filled with the stuff for reptilian brains?"

If you see an ad associated with a product, it is more than likely connected to a warehouse full of the product. The company fears losing a lot of money if they do not sell it soon. Instead of sending some *thing* for Christmas this year, why not make available your intimately sharing self?

The Return of Intimacy

For several years, Max and I downsized Christmas. Then one year, we didn't have it. We all survived just fine, playing games together, laughing, and generally enjoying each other. During one of those years, on the way to not having Christmas, we celebrated with a "half" of a Christmas tree in the house. We found it at a tree farm, abandoned in the middle of the field. They looked surprised when we asked what they wanted for the little Christmas tree with only one side. "Uh, five dollars," they said hesitantly. "We'll take it."

At home, I decorated the side that had few branches with varying lengths of fish line, attached to clear glass ornaments. I decorated the other side with the lights and colored ornaments. It was stunning, and it reflected the philosophy my husband and I share, that holy caring restores beauty to things that have been hurt. In our beliefs, abuse and losses do not win over the love and caring God teaches us. I have decorated many trees, but that one stands out in my memory.

It is the acceptance of a Greater Life Force than our own small microcosmic and biologic reactions that opens us to the high of the heart. Balance is about having all of life's responses present in healthy proportions, and not about trying to substitute one for the other.

When the death of a loved one happens in the life of a person with imbalance between their nurturing and primitive responses, the receiving place for a blessed death is small indeed. This person will tend to categorize the coming death into crisis or nuisance. They have no history of a beautiful, slow and sweetly intimate, peace-filled, graciously built, final time with a loved one. Without a chemical high of their brain, they are feeling bored, or as if they are wasting time.

In contrast, time is suspended during the high of the heart. There is no need that cannot be met calmly. As mom died, her strength and presence of her gentle, faith-filled life poured out, undiluted, into the room. I am so grateful that I had the receiving place for this. Her chemistry parted ways as her mind, body and spirit took different paths to meet her dying needs. The only requirement from her family became one of simply being...as we watched her being come to a close.

The topics of our chemistry are mostly held in separate pieces of knowledge. If you know something about the medicines you take, or how exercise affects you, or about your individual imbalances, such as migraine headaches, diabetis, or allergies, you have some of the pieces. You may question: Is this just another topic too big and clumsy to fully absorb regarding my individual needs? Maybe, but beyond the individual responsibility there is a broader influence chemistry is making on our environment.

As a child I enjoyed watching the crop dusters that flew close to my house spraying the pesticide, DDT. Did that DDT, a chemical now banned from use in the United States, have any long term effects on my health? Were my continual colds as a child, or my own son's birth defects related in any way to DDT? What are the chemical inferences behind my inability to use most antibiotics? Or my extreme sensitivity now to bug sprays, or strong perfumes?

William was born before my (former) husband went

to Viet Nam and was exposed to Agent Orange. Besides the devastating side effects he has suffered, to what extent has my daughter been exposed, who was conceived after Viet Nam?

If the County Hospital Psychiatric ward had managed to keep my father's murderer under medication for his paranoid schizophrenia, how might my life have been different? If the psychiatrist had not allowed him to leave the hospital against medical advice that day, would he still have found a way to kill my father? If my mother had not believed so strongly in her medicines, and taken them so faithfully, would she still have lived twenty years with heart disease? If I had not healed so much from my anger, would my personal chemistry have blocked my reception of my mother's grace-filled death?

The "whys" I mentioned before seem to also be tied into questions related to Chemistry. It seems my ability to cope, to live, and even to thrive are inter-related with the understanding of my chemistry. I cannot afford to *not* know something about the chemistry, and yet there is so much we still don't know.

Finding balance to our thoughts includes knowing ourselves well enough to see the effects of loss on our minds and hearts, our chemistry, and our well-being. When we are side-tracked by the greed in our culture to feed the frenzy of our reptilian brains, we side-step our more tender inclinations to nurture meaningful community.

Count on it -- if your mental math is off, your chemistry is off, and you are in danger of suffering the consequences from the inevitable glitch in your thinking. To redirect yourself, and come back to feeling alive, you will need to grieve. I call it grief work.

To be alive is

To be growing and changing,
To be creating and unfolding
To fully seek the Yahweh, I am
To be alive is to be --
Fully present for the gifts
Deposited in each moment.
To be alive is to find real pain and
Continue anyway to be grateful and
Hopeful for the promises of life.
To be alive is to know
Losses happen
Inevitably
To feel alive
requires
Telling truth
Truth of the past
Truth of the present
Throughout tough lessons
Remembering our path
Flowing from the past
Spirit, Mind and Body
Wellness and connection
Sharing Safe Intimacy

-kAh-

FIVE

Grief Work

The process of grieving is referred to as doing ones *grief work*. It seems right to call grief "work," because it is emotionally and energetically exhausting. Not to be confused with physical labor, grief work can be done while chopping wood or running a fast two miles, but it is better defined as telling your story to an open and caring listener.

In the honoring of telling your true story,
- you have a voice
- you hear your voice
- and you have a witness.

Speaking and hearing your true voice acts as self-validation, and having a witness provides validation from others. A witness may not always agree with you, but they leave out judgment and condemnation during this time of holy listening. Truth, honor, self-validation, and validation from others are all essential components within the healing process.

Grief often trumps other emotions, and can surface with a sight, a sound, or a fragrance. These "triggers" can suddenly transform the current experience to one of remembering another time and place. Feeling the emotions when they come, rather than stuffing them, allows the work of remembering. Remembering helps to restore the deceased loved one into our long term living memory, especially if you can talk about it, and continue to feel safely vulnerable.

People often fear grieving. They don't want to begin to feel their pain, for fear they will "never stop crying" once they begin. Or, "nothing will get better", "the loss will still be there" when they finish. What most people don't know is that yes, the loss will still be there -- the pain will not.

Restoration after a loss becomes painfree remembering. Telling both the good and bad stories will create a solid memory of a loved one, rather than a frighteningly fading one. Doing your grief work brings the gift of restoring a loved one to your life. It is in our healing that we find a release from the pain of loss. I have provided some examples in this book with the stories of my own losses. As readers, you are my additional witnesses, and I thank you.

My Story

My father died on September 5th, 1968. It was a year of assassinations, civil rights movements, riots and unrest. My father's murder was a variation on these bloody themes, but much less public than the deaths of Martin Luther King, Jr. and Bobby Kennedy, who were also killed in 1968.

In June of 1968, I remember carrying my three-day old son home from a military hospital in Germany, when I heard the news of Robert Kennedy's assassination in the U.S. We were back in the United States when Dad was killed, three months later. The need for law and order appears to be part of my son's personal constitution; today he is a policeman.

Who can say how much it is a reflection of the timing of his birth. 1968 was a violently, out-of-control year.

On September 6, 2003, my mother died, twelve hours and 35 years after my father. She died in an integrated nursing home, having been treated by many specialists and doctors, including one from Iran. As she lay dying, Mom was visited by her granddaughter, just home from the Peace Corps. My mother lived beyond, and subsequently died in a different world than the one we knew in 1968. Hard-fought-for changes separated the three decades. We were all different, certainly older, maybe wiser, more cynical, more experienced, and oddly enough, both more and less tolerant.

On the day she died, the front page of the newspaper carried a picture of a marine, home from the war in Iraq. His parents are pastors of the Hispanic Weslyan Church in town. If this person would have been considered newsworthy at all in the late 60's, he would probably have been on the back page. The 2003 newspaper gave equal space and a neutral tone to the class project studying homosexuality at the University, a seven-year study on the effects of poverty on state-mandated test scores, and free bug spray, along with instructions in Spanish to help citizens fight West Nile disease carried by mosquitos.

Sadly, some have died so that we could live more equally, openly, and honestly in 2003. The positive changes have come slowly, and only on certain kinds of things. The differences, however, appeared obvious to me when my two parents died 35 years apart. In addition to my two biological parents, my step father died from Parkinson's Disease, with dementia, in 1994. More often than not, my experiences with death have fallen toward the extremes.

Mom's death, on the positive end of this spectrum, introduced a new and magnificent choice that profoundly defined the discreet exit points of the mind, body, and soul. Dad's death brought such a crushing blow that it nearly obliterated all possibilities of understanding along with it, and my stepfather faded away. Each death represents a different experience along death's continuum.

Violent Death

In 1968, I was twenty-one, and the blow to my psyche and essence radically altered the direction of my life. I felt as if my heart had been sliced in half, and I was supposed to learn to live while I, personally, continued to slowly bleed to death. I saw no end to my pain. I suppose that parts of my life are irretrievably folded in the gray matter of my brain. There's no telling what all I've done to cope with the level of fear and terror that attached itself to my insides then and for many years following the time of Dad's death.

Dad was murdered by a paranoid schizophrenic person with such brutality that I played the tape of it in my head for 28 years, until one day it occurred to me to go and view the "real" pictures in the police report. Mercifully, this activity rid me of the loop of film in my mind's eye that kept repeating the act of his murder. Instead, the act of brutality flattened out into a black and white photo, more bloody than I had imagined, but easier to live with. It is a file I can retrieve by choice, but no longer a tape that rolls ad nauseum through my head. My unresolved and unfinished imaginings went away when the truth came with resolution.

An Answer in Grace

That day, that Mom and I went through the file together, I let die my obligation to keep my father's murder alive in my brain. I am not certain if it was a choice, or if *grace* dissolved it, as rain dissolves salt. Perhaps it was a combination of choice and grace. I consider it grace when one remembers the truth, and yet it is no longer painful. Grace brings freedom from the pain.

Finding grace, often a shortcut through our worst nightmares, may resemble a search for a secret passage. While spiritual sustenance is the source of our answers, it can evade us, especially when the messages to us are mixed. I have experienced such confusion, and sent my own mixed messages at times. Afterall, as extremely as Dad's death affected me, Mom's death had an opposite and equal effect. Since her death, a marvelous sense of balance has remained with me. Between the time of Dad's death and her own, Mom seemed to find additional faith and grace for her toolbox for living. Thankfully, she brought them to her dying experience.

Perhaps Dad had tools, but I wasn't there, and it all happened so fast. Something tells me that he did experience grace, but from the other side of the veil. I have wondered for years. So much unthinkable, unfathomable mystery was around Dad's death. On the other hand, Mom's death seemed to clear away the secrets that had been hidden from my view. Clarity, answers, and grace walked in and sat with us for days, with the unfolding honor of being at Mom's side during such a holy time.

Mom lived 85 years, mostly modeling a loving

kindness, acceptance of others, and a routinely gentle and productive life. She was surely one of the subtlest feminists I have ever known, but there is no denying that she was one. She approached her death much the way she approached her life, out of this strength of character and mind. I am proud to have witnessed her life.

I am not certain what fueled my mother's perpetual energy. When she was young, I remember her literally running through her day. Mom reminded me of the pink bunny battery, constantly going. Dad would say, "Slow down, Mrs. A. You'll live longer."

Then ironically he died first, and too early, just shy of 52. I thought Mom would work herself into her grave then. After a string of continuous activities, committees, church, traveling, and volunteering years after retiring from a thirty year librarian career, the quiet alterations of her structured world and her worn body led her to finally wind down. She slowed down, largely because her legs got tired, having been stripped of their veins for her open-heart, bypass surgery. Her routines continued the way a clock would continue to go around the numbers, slowly losing time.

Thirteen hours before she died, she called her final committee meeting. She requested a discussion of her funeral service, with her pastor, my husband, and myself. She was pleased to know that we would be following the instructions she had left us, and that in addition, all sets of families would participate. I smile when I think that the final satisfying activity of my mother was to make a plan, especially for the final memories her loved ones would have of her.

In contrast to the many details I remember about my mother's funeral, I remember only five things from my dad's service: seeing him in a casket, the spring-green dress I wore, the family in a huge circle as they prayed together in our front yard before we left for the church, walking down the aisle of the church, and the hollow feeling of complete devastation actively carving out my insides.

Since burying Mother, remembering her has produced predominantly celebratory emotions, despite the usual absent-mindedness to pick up the phone and call her, and the sadness that follows the realization that I cannot call her. I have been rejoicing in both her life and her death, as if she gifted me a full, rich treasure chest of memories and one priceless pearl I hold inside my heart. The awe-filled night of her passing, like a gentle meditation, rests serenely in my mind, along with the scent of the burning vanilla candle and the fragrance of red roses wafting on the late summer breeze coming through the open window.

So strong and available were our feelings of love for her, that we could stroke her arms and legs as they grew colder. We clearly witnessed her body's final attempts to survive, as it drew back her blood to her most vital internal organs, her heart and her lungs. As the end neared, I was able to rock her in my arms, and whisper "bye-bye." I treasure the moment her childlike voice echoed "bye-bye" back to me. We did this in succession three times, a sweet and final song of death. It seemed her Spirit left with these words, and not long after that, she stopped breathing.

I am grateful to God and to my mother for the incredible gift of living right into her dying, and for providing part of the answer to the question of how does one make the dying experience full of life right up to the end of one's time of being together.

Despite Mom repeatedly saying, "I don't know how to do this," somehow, she did. This is the record of how it seemed to me that death came peacefully into our lives.

But before peace, there was anger. I coped by being angry for a much longer part of my grieving than would have had to be, had I received better counseling. Five counselors I paid and prayed for for help, were not trained in the healing of trauma. I was to live decades before finding the understanding of my coping mechanisms to trauma.

Anger

I am as happy now with my mother as, oppositionally, I was angry with my father -- for years. How dare he die! How dare he strip us of his loving presence! How stupidly he behaved -- to go to a known psychopath's home alone, and let himself be murdered! Believe me, I've worked hard to not be that ignorant, to not be alone with an insane person, and to not get stupidly dead!

In the beginning this anger served me well. It helped me to feel alive, in that I was so numb, and so much in shock from the devastating murder of my father. Anger was something I knew how to feel. My anger served as a container for my emotions of emptiness, confusion, sadness, resentment, and the pain of loss. Cloaked by anger, it was all I knew. Other emotions were strangers. Eventually, under an illusion of control, my anger festered into pockets of puss that helped to destroy my marriage, my health, and my future. Of course, I didn't know it at the time.

Now I am aware that angry judgment is a great temptor, but a lousy teacher, and no lover of life. If one adds righteous indignation to angry judgment, you have the cocktail I drank of daily, for years. It provided an emotional, chemical, religious barrier to the pain inside, and unknowingly, to others outside.

Left on its own, anger takes one of two directions. It goes inward, or it comes outward. Anger turned inward is usually experienced as depression, or physical illness. Anger turned outward can become rage. Angry people see themselves differently than others see them, but you'll recognize the pincushion and cactus characteristics when you see them. Whether they voice it or not, angry people often feel both guilt and blame, and most certainly feel disunited inside, and disconnected from others on the outside.

Whether aimed in or out, the angry person usually perceives their anger at least to be justified, if not also a protection from pain. This concept of anger having a by-product of safe community is terribly wrong math. (Remember the glitch?) At times being angry awakens our need for change in our lives. In a brief blast, anger can alert others to danger, but the truly constructive use of anger is not longlasting.

Mixing anger into my verbal gift produced razor-sharp words that helped me to protect (or so I thought) myself and my loved ones from "unreasonable wrong." Perhaps I reasoned, albeit subconsciously, that the pain from a thousand slicing words was no more than the namby-pamby pain of a few years of bleeding cuticles, which was nothing, compared to my heart's torturous pain of violently and immediately losing someone I loved, as much as I loved my father.

I coped with the death of my father without a teacher, a mentor, a counselor, or even a best friend. Like two blind persons taking a dinghy over Niagra Falls, my mother and I clung to each other, ignorantly unskilled to handle such rough waters of grief. We could not have known that our losses were more than simply emotional.

The losses were spiritually profound, mentally explosive, and physically chemically scalding. Trauma definitively splits out of the need to self-preserve the mind from the body from the spirit. Nature's plan is that at least one of the parts will survive.

The lengthier explanations of trauma fall outside the scope of this book. Eventually those of us who have been traumatized (if we live long enough) do realize that something in our lives has to change. We "wake up to smell the coffee." We realize that death is here to stay, and it is a part of life. Unfortunately, even violent, abrupt death is here to stay, even though it is wrong, terribly wrong.

Sooner or later, I had to distinguish between the natural anger of losing a loved one, and taking out my self-righteous anger on others because I had been wronged. Just as my dad (and maybe yours too) had said, "Two wrongs don't make a right." This is to say that eventually I had to come to grips with being a victim. Whether the bullet goes through the right side, or the left side of the brain -- victimization is --

Victimization

We have all been victims, when taken in the context of mankind. The screaming parent, physical abuse, a violent sexual assault, the terror of a violent crime, a car crash, the murder that strips a person of life on an otherwise normal afternoon, and suicide from the temporarily paralyzed mind, are all victimizations that victimize more than the victim. The survivors and the witnesses also suffer.

It is from this place of suffering that victims feel helpless to change things, and it is from helplessness to change that we seed our largest fields of anger. Anger becomes a tough surface, under which helplessness leaves a decaying infrastructure. Like termites rotting out the floors and walls; we miss the helplessness underneath the anger until someone or something "falls through."

Huge warning signs abound in our nation, of the increased sense of helplessness, camouflaged by angry, violent acts of humans against humans, sometimes ones they love. My father had befriended the man who killed him. Most violence in our nation happens between people who know each other.

Reading through the police report on my father's death took about (28 years to think of doing it and) an hour to actually read through it. Page after page of treatment plans from review boards represented the court case that never happened, because the man who killed Dad was "innocent by reason of insanity." The three decades since his death were summarized in a folder about three inches thick. That's an inch per decade, I guess. Dad's killer was in a mental holding pattern, supposedly suspended in his mind's loss of memory of his brutal actions. And then there were the photographs --of something I had only imagined countless times.

There was my sweet and gentle father, silent and bloody, never to laugh with me again. Gone forever as my teacher and guide, loving parent, father-like-mother (home each afternoon after school), flower-growing, chicken-raising, corny and kind person. Gone, gone, gone, gone, along with his murderer's memory. It was never as easy as just getting up and walking out of a bad movie, nor turning off the nightly newscast about a local homicide.

A strange (but not unusual) paradox is this need to see a memory more clearly and more accurately in order to heal from the painful partial view. Now, my visual of Dad's death is a single, one-dimensional, black and white photo that I have a choice of whether or not to view. The loop I played for years indicated a need for something, in my case information, the retrieval of which served to help me heal.

Anger is a winding river. If navigated too long, you may reach the falls. You may be angry about the timing of your loved ones unavoidable death. You may feel indignant that you didn't see it coming, or that they didn't, or that they should have, or that this shouldn't happen to you.

Sure, we all have to die, but not now, especially not now...

The timing of losses can be massively unfair, especially that of a parent, a child, a spouse, a partner or best friend. We need these people to be alive and here for us. We need them to remind us to feel alive, and well, and important, and needed. They filled a place no one else can fill.

Like the smell of the fish docks can distract us from the beauty of the ocean, anger can distract us from the blessing and the beauty of death. Consider thoughtfully whether or not you bring anger to a person you love who is in the process of dying. Are you bringing any of the following symptoms of anger to your loved one:

a) a need for immediacy?

b) an impatience with this person's timing and the interruption into your own life by their dying?

c) anger or frustration, with underlying hopelessness or helplessness (perhaps about their situation, medication, choices of doctors, where they are living, or something else you don't understand)?

d) personal chemical habits of anger, lust, overeating, smoking, drinking, self-starving, or numbing?

e) unresolved issues with this person?

f) ignorance and confusion?

Or, are you bringing a calm receptivity, and hope for a kind and gentle closure? There is still time, probably, for sorting some of this out. The person dying may be experiencing a range of these angry feelings also. There will be opportunity to resolve some of the anger and pain of previous losses, as you learn about death together, as you both move toward letting go of each other. Many people will suggest that you "let go, and let God." The truly angry, wounded person won't (really can't) let go until several things are in place.

Letting Go of Anger

1. <u>Spiritual willingness and trust need to be in place.</u> Sometimes this is complicated, as it was in my case. The man who murdered Dad reported that God told him to do it. Apparently, he thought he was Jesus Christ, and that Dad was the devil, and that's why he had to be destroyed the way he was. I was more than thirteen years sorting that part out. (See *Spirit*, page 131)

2. <u>The truth of the victimization needs to be clearly understood and stated to an empathetic and non-judgmental witness.</u> The act of sharing the truth helps the victim to

move into becoming a survivor.

3. Survivors have the hard work of <u>restoring their sense of identity and authority,</u> without the puffed-up presence of either arrogance or anger, or the contamination of victimization to their original sense of innocence. Often this process requires a mentor, pastor, or therapist to help you do this.

When you can speak to the wrongness of a violation, with a sense of strength, conviction, and accuracy, but without slipping into the victim emotions of anger and helplessness, you have probably found your personal sense of authority.

Truth remains after pain. It resides in your understanding of who you are, despite what has happened to you. It resonates from the center of your body, coming up into your voice, authoring your truth to others. Have someone put a hand on the center of your back and then speak your truth from the place where their hand rests. You will hear the difference yourself when you speak calmly, and truthfully from this central place, representing personal honor, dignity, and authority.

Authority happens as a result of pro-actively seeking healing. It assists in the pain of remembering your truth, voicing your pain, searching your current needs, and sharing your vulnerability with others who are safe. It resonates from the center of your wellness, aligned with your chronological age. It reflects the recovered maturity, grateful heart, and mended being. No one can force themselves into their authorship; we heal into that place through a holy path.

4. Accompanying a sense of authority, you will begin <u>to feel okay to live</u> (either for the first time or to live again). People violated when very young have to LEARN to live. Because I was wounded at the doorway of my adult years,

I actually had never experienced being fully adult, without the contamination of also being wounded. Only after my healing, well into my adult years, could I become an adult living free of the pain of the wounds. This was complicated by over twenty moves and other profoundly deep losses. I needed most of every minute in those three decades to "grow up," in order to have some form of readiness for my mother to die two years ago!

5. The crowning level of life is <u>warrior</u>, but listen carefully. If your history is that of victimization, you will walk in your suffering until you recognize your painful wounds. Upon recognition, you will begin the difficult, truth-sharing path of the survivor. During this time, you must learn how to live beyond the defining moments of your painful history. Healing will help you to emerge happy, serene, and able to discuss your history clearly and with little pain. Throughout this process of learning who you really are (neither a victim nor a survivor originally), your holy gifts will begin to be seen.

<u>The surrendering of ones gifts to be used by God</u> happens from the place of authority (wisely, not sooner). This is when God invites you into the larger calling of being his warrior. It is both a gentle and powerful place, with all the characteristics of 1 Corinthians 13... filled with love only God can do, and He finds a way to do it through you. It is humbling, confusing, and humanly impossible to maintain, so this level of growth becomes a repeated surrendering to the Higher Power. It is here we see that life is about a complicated and continual action of letting go.

Most wounded persons will be challenged to step into something that approximates these levels of growth. I have experienced this healing process and witnessed this healing process many, many times in others. However I may be blessed in my dying, I believe it will be one more lesson in "letting go, and letting God." There are many doorways (I suppose into the many mansions) so I am not suggesting any one way to accomplish these levels of growth. I put it this way with clients: "God built the blueprint for healing inside of you, all we have to do is access it." My only advice at this juncture is *"whatever you do, remember to breathe."*

Shared Grief Work

The work of grief is remembering, and it doesn't all have to be done after someone dies. In fact, it was easier for Mom and friends and family who were able, to do some grieving with her. Two days before she died, an associate from the library, and dear friend for years, came by and reminisced for more than an hour. As they finished each other's sentences, the rest of us listened with delight, to the shared memories of these two trail-blazing women. My mother and her successor were responsible for libraries and bookmobiles making their way into many small, rural Northern Colorado towns.

We were amazed that Mother could rally so, and fully participate. It was a fun and joyful hour, discrediting the idea that all grief is painful. Grief is about remembering everything -- the good, the bad, and the glue inbetween. We appear less worrisome about remembering the good, but it is equally as important for the purpose of solidifying the memory of a loved one into wholeness that lives on into the future with us.

Balance within the grief work is essential in order

to arrive eventually, if not to a sense of completion, at least to a sense of having grieved enough. That is why so many recommendations from the 12 Step programs work to help people to grieve. Taking one day at a time, minding your own business, not trying to take someone else's inventory, sharing your truth, listening attentively when others speak, seeking your Higher Power -- all help to bring renewal along with balance. If you do not understand the meanings of these phrases, I invite you to consider attending a 12 Step Anonymous Group. If there has been any addiction in your life, pick the anonymous group that matches the closest with your issues. If you have lived with an addict, Al-Anon is a good place to begin. CODA (Codependency Anonymous) groups focus on getting your attentions back to meeting your own needs first. This is not about being selfish, but rather about grabbing that oxygen mask that just dropped in front of your face before you attempt to help another put on their oxygen mask. You won't be any good to someone else if you are passed out cold.

Search for a grief support group until you find one. Look for a church that understands the long, painful path grief sometimes takes. Look for a therapist who has experience as a bereavement counselor. Look for group leaders who have led others from the darkness that surrounds loss. Look for listeners. Listen to others. Share without judgment and comparison whenever possible.

Loss is Loss

L oss is painful. It lacks consideration. It gulps great chunks of time, produces brain fog, and wears gray continually, until you want to scream for a vivid hot pink, a scratchy sound bite, an exotic fragrance, or an outrageous thunderstorm, whose lightning will disrupt the electricity that runs the obsessive thoughts of your mind. Too dramatic? Maybe. But, we can't actually see loss, so what we see is a person's skills at grieving. (We see their interpretation of their loss.)

We can only resonate with someone else's loss. Loss is an individual experience for which we have no witness, but God. We can only communicate about losses through the demonstration, understanding, and sharing of our own experiences. It is not wise to try to pretend about this knowledge or understanding.

It is better to say, "I do not understand what you are having to go through," in truth, than to say any of the thousands of things people say to others who are in their dreadful pain of loss. To read some of the "dumbest things people can say" to widows and widowers, go to the Internet web site www.widownet.org. You may hear some anger from the recipients of these comments, who have to find not only a way to live with their pain, but a way to live with the insensitivity of others who think they should just "get over it," or quickly "move on."

Despite the saying, "misery loves company," grief actually does better with a loving, empathetic listener, on an "as-needed" basis. Getting inside another's circle of grief can lead to enmeshment, that may create a dependency.

However, going away from the grieving person, out of your own discomfort, will likely result in their feelings of increased losses. If a person feels their friends and family members don't talk to them about their situation, they may feel (yet another) abandonment. The essential balance is especially hard to find in the situation of having a care giver and a care receiver.

The teeter-totter may pivot on the losses instead of renegotiating the joy of living around a simpler life. When the care receiver is bitter, the care giver often feels damned if they do, and damned if they don't. Both "sides" feel lonely when blame and defensiveness frame the experience. The loneliness may be grief over losses accumulated over the years, that have never been resolved.

It is not uncommon for a distance to grow between you and your loved one. You are walking the path toward inevitable separation, and separate unknown futures. The feelings of anxiety and panic are not uncommon. Former familiar coping strategies come charging to the rescue, only to feel futile and dissatisfying. Attempts to *make* things happen may be disastrous, yet continued denial that *something* is happening may cheat your blessings. It is possible that you never needed more help in your life, but possibly never felt less like asking for it.

However, this is the time to bring in more troops. **Seek help**. Get more information, a neutral other set of eyes and ears, evaluation from professionals, respite care, support. (See Part II: Encouragement for Caregivers.) Start with one question a day, outside of your own knowledge base.

Least helpful, perhaps, is the act of worrying. While worrying does seem to derive from the compassionate nature, it appears to be bogged down and usually ineffective compassion. As the antithesis of living in the present moment, worry is usually based upon fears of the future. When you worry, you have little power to stay connected to the truth of the current situation. Your fears and feelings are engaged with an unknown future, possibly mixed with the unresolved past. The perception feels so inevitable that the imagined thoughts seem sure to happen. Furthermore, worrying can turn into obsessive thinking, one of the least constructive kinds of thought.

Appendix B (page 178) extends this dialogue about living with less worry and fear. A therapist, see Appendix C (page 180) for helping you find one, should be able to help you to identify those things keeping you from satisfactorily living with your current situation.

If someone is sick and possibly dying, staying present is especially important. If you imagine funerals, hospital visits, wrecks, or accidents to the point that your imagination and your sense of pain interfere with your real life, you definitely want to seek some active (probably professional) help toward becoming current and real.

Perhaps these worries represent unresolved historic incidents that really happened to you, and of course, some of them may happen in the future. Worrying about things that are not happening at this time, and may or may not happen ever, however, is a huge waste of your precious life.

The need to learn about the work of grieving will come with each new loss, so it often feels "endless." Isn't breathing endless? Don't we have to continue to eat, in order to live? Aging, changing, moving through transitions, adapting, and yes, grieving all have qualities of being on-going. I invite you to learn to do them all as well as you can. In order to live the zestful and joy-filled life, it is my experience that first I had to learn to live steadily and quietly with serenity.

SIX

Living with Serenity

Core beliefs produce assumptions that are foundational to your decisions of whether or not to commit to something. If your core belief is that you are loved and loving, your commitments will reflect this belief. Your behaviors come out of your commitments, and a peaceful community comes out of your behaviors. Or not.

Who wouldn't choose serenity over unrest, irritation, anger, and sadness? Who wouldn't choose calm and cheerfulness over a panic or anxiety disorder? Oversimplifying the difficulties of living seldom helps anyone over the humps, and in fact usually creates more moguls to maneuver on the downhill slope.

Feeling whole and integrated is not just imagined; these are threads that begin with core beliefs and find their way to the surface in actions. Some parts of the core beliefs are established as early on as pre-verbal instances of being held and loved in safety as an infant. Integrity and consistency within a child's environment of receiving loving, peaceful nurturance will produce integrity and consistency within the adult whose role is suddenly reversed with a parent who is increasingly childlike. In such cases, peace flows from the wholeness and self-acceptance naturally, even when it needs to happen in reversed roles.

In persons who did not receive a sense of being loved, or loved conditionally (only if they are good enough, smart enough, religious enough, and pretty enough, for example) small dips in the chemistry can find their way toward downward spirals. The emotional journey can be dominated by plummeting.

Attempts to continually shelve thoughts about deaths and losses, usually sooner -- rather than later, reflect an imbalance. The imbalance is of course exacerbated by additional chemical and emotional spins played out by fears, hormones, low self-esteem, acting out, acting in, and dis-ease. The disease construct comes from the lack-of-ease of living (dis-ease).

Discomfort, unhappiness, sadness, anger, shock, frustration, confusion may tend to be addressed as "something to fix" by the time you decide to give them your attention. Strong emotions are naturally part of the grieving process, but not necesssarily at the level most people finally acknowledge their presence. If you're wise, you don't wait to put oil in the car until black smoke is pouring out of the tail pipe.

So where is the balance? How much thinking about death and dying is healthy? When might chronically sick conditions in the body reflect an unwillingness to integrate gains and losses? Most importantly, when is it the right time to accept death peacefully as opposed to fight off the end of life -- and for how long, a day, six months, a year? How can anyone find answers to the difficult questions of life, unless they are first asking the questions?

Beginning with two assumptions "we are all dying," and "dying peacefully is the best way to die," may help to produce an internal commitment toward living a peaceful life on a daily basis. It is a beginning place.

I believe that the complement of living serenely into our experience of dying will create a fuller, freer sense of life, all along the way. As you attempt to live daily with serenity, you may begin to notice how captivating life really can be. The flowers have more color; the food a better taste; friendships feel more meaningful; family members more dear. The goal, in other words, is to feel the same serenity about both living and dying. Living is not easy; dying is not simple. Watching my mother over the years come into the fullness of doing both well, provided me the template for hoping for the best for myself and others.

When her winter came, and the leaves dropped from the trees, I saw the outline of the larger mountain -- serenity. It rose above the valley of death in grandeur, still part of a single range, on a bigger continent. I knew her death was not just about one woman's interpretation. This was the tranquil, loving gift abiding in her life for years. Mom approached dying conjoined with living. Being unafraid to grieve was the glue.

Finding the Time to Grieve

If you need to grieve, and you need to work to pay the bills during the same time period, it will be hard to find the time and energy to grieve properly. There are not many short-cuts to the grieving process. It will always require some time and attention to grieve, but small, manageable moments of grieving can still help. Here are some brief ways to allow grief an inroad to healing:

   - Take a ten minute quiet break for yourself, daily.

   - Allow yourself feelings for brief times during the day.

   - Promise yourself that you will return to grieving later, at a specific time -- and then meet your promise.

   - Be realistic about your need to have some time alone.

   - Say "No" when you don't want to be around people.

   - Say "No" when you would rather be with people, but you have a real sense of needing to do some solitary grieving.

   - Don't beat yourself up about being in a fog, that's grief.

   - See a doctor if you think you are also depressed.

   - Take some time to read about others in your situation.

   - Take as much time as you need to learn to flow with life again. If others have advice who haven't lived what you have lived through, tell them, "Thanks, I know you mean well, but I am pretty certain our experiences are not the same."

   - Seek professional help that may expedite the process.

   - Avoid substitutions (i.e. alcohol) in lieu of doing grief work, and finally, know that your healing is not completely dependent on how well you do this. Thankfully, God is bigger than any of us. Remember, a glitch in your thinking will **substitute** things and actions for taking time to grieve. My own story of substituting too much of something for not enough of something else began with losing Rena.

Losing Rena

I lost my first-born child thirty-eight years ago. I grieved her loss deeply, and when my happiness returned I thought I had betrayed her. Today, at the most, I might grieve her loss once or twice a year, and then usually when I am speaking with a young mother who has deep pain over a miscarriage, a premature baby who has died, or a stillborn infant. I realize, in this connection, that my grief will never completely go away, because it is a life memory. The tears flow with the empathy I feel. However, they are usually accompanied by very little personal pain.

I believe it is healthy living to move beyond the sense of embarrassment, and to grieve in the company of others. In this case, my grieving is with the young mother with the fresher, and more acute pain. Not only do I become her community in the moment, but the moment also becomes a cleansing for me. It has an unscheduled arrival time. I don't fight it. Until it happens, it's not really on my mind. When it shows up, I am neither surprised nor upset with the tears that come so easily to my eyes.

I remember Rena -- small, pink, and perfect, except for the lungs that would not support her need to breathe. She was born in Germany, and no family members were there to comfort or guide us. My husband and I were the only ones at the burial of our first born child. We stood together on the side of a beautiful German mountain, at a loss for both words and ceremony. We paid for her cremation, and her ashes were housed in a small black metal ball, no larger than a softball. We had to buy a shovel. I thought burying her ashes in Germany would leave the pain there, but afterward not one bit of the pain in my gut had moved. I carried it forward for years. No joy and no sorrow could replace my need to grieve.

No one taught us how to grieve this loss. My husband pushed it behind his work and alcohol, and we wavered between arguing, feeling stunned, and surviving in angry silence. The chemical, downward spiral began in both of us, further aggravated by more deaths (including that of my father) and several other losses during the next five years. Looking back, I am grateful to have survived. However, what took years to heal might have healed sooner had I known then what I know now about the process of grieving.

For starters, I didn't know about the glitch, and its wrong math in my thinking. I didn't know society was attempting to teach me that more money will fix feelings of loss or lonliness; that more (or less) sex will fix a disturbed relationship; that the lack of intimate sharing within a marriage can be replaced by a more demanding work load; that the loss of a loved one will be relieved by a pill, chocolate, or cleaning. Following this line of reasoning would lead a person to believe one could pour enough gasoline inside a car to make it clean, or that if you shop enough you can change how you feel about yourself. Do these sound ridiculous, or at least wrong? Many such distortions perpetuate the fine art of avoidance of pain.

Listening to others, and not knowing any better, I followed ways of avoiding consideration of my pain. It was years before I realized how important Rena's 27 hour life and her 38 year death would be to me. She's important today, because remembering her is the next right thing here.

The Long Road

Finding serenity is only possible when the puzzle pieces are identified. If you are clinically depressed, you will probably feel better taking an anti-depressant, because you may bring a better chemical balance into your body. Taking chemistry to balance chemistry is sensible math. If, however, an underlying cause of the upheaval in your chemistry is a lack of appropriate grieving, the next loss will throw off the formula. On this theory, eventually you would need a pill the size of a football. As Adele Davis once wrote, "Why not, a python can swallow a pig."

The thing I thought most often when I lost my father at the age of 21 was, "He is the one person who could explain this to me. He would know how to comfort me. He's the one gone; this is so unfair." It took me years to find the tools to use, but first I tried what the culture taught me -- to mask grief, swallow it along with something sweet or strong, ignore it, fake it, hide it, or stay busy seeking distractions.

These are still the most popular ways to deal with losses. Perhaps one of my generation's greatest challenges is before us now. In this our final quarter of a century (if we are lucky) we can identify ways of letting go with dignity, defining simpler and more meaningful lives, strengthening our relationships with those we will leave behind, and grieving our inevitable losses with courage and balance.

It is our task to begin to change this culturally accepted error in our thinking. Honesty about the pain of losses will begin to correct our course. In addition to our wealth of plans and ideas, our money, our retirement and our accumulation of material goods, let us leave a gift of compassionate foresight. Let us leave the legacy of what and how to grieve.

We need to grieve the losses of youth to drugs and suicide. We need to grieve the losses to violent crimes. We need to grieve the loss of safety in schools and the lives of young people. We need to grieve what we have lost to the speed of living too fast a life. We need to grieve the numbers of deaths by drunk drivers. We need to grieve the rape and sexual abuse in our country. We need to grieve the loss of hope and faith. We need to grieve our unavailability to each other. We need to grieve or we will perish under the crushing burden of hate and bitterness, numbness to pain, absence of hope, and low self-esteem that comes in the wake of our not grieving. Worse yet, the fallout from our lack of grieving will be generations even further distanced from their pain.

As you learn to grieve, consider how you will share the grieving process with those you will leave behind. Open, truthful grieving is needed so that love and intimacy have space and room to grow in your heart. This is the only road I've found to living with serenity on a daily basis.

The Premise

I have mentioned the characteristics of grief and the importance of learning to resolve and live with your losses. You may have glanced at the Appendices. You may have started jotting down a few ideas. Or you may have felt so overwhelmed by this discussion on a topic you hardly want to read or talk about to begin with, that you either fell asleep, skipped a lot, or put the book down several times already.

If you are absolutely perky, congratulate yourself on your healthy state (or complete denial). A wounded logic keeps us from moving through emotionally painful work. Wounded logic is packed full of wrong assumptions that lead us to believe that no amount of painful remembering will heal us or make us feel better. However, the premise under which I am writing believes that healing can happen. Yes, grief, death, and losses will continue to be part of living, but while working through these things can be painful (and often labor intensive), healing can bring us to a transcended level of freedom from the pain.

Take some time to think about what you are reading, and exactly how it relates to you now. This will give you the greatest benefit in the long run. Meditation, study, prayer, and quiet time all help us to focus away from daily frustrations, worries, and distractions, into a peaceful, energetic, hope-filled, healing place. This is where you will access your blueprint to heal. Here are a few more hints to help you in this process:

a) On a journey, the terrain is *never always* anything; the journey moves from hills to valleys to plains.

b) You will have better recall of this information for future use if you write some notes to yourself, answer some of the questions, journal, or discuss some of the chapters with others. (Feel free to duplicate the questions from the Appendices for group discussions.)

c) If you received this book from a hospice or hospital, please discuss and read parts of it with the loved one who is possibly dying soon. The chapters on *Wellness, Family,* and *Preparation* might work as ice breakers.

d) Thinking in terms of process, not product, is essential. We are never finished with ourselves, until the living is finished... and even then, in the end, we've probably finished a chapter, not the whole book.

e) Write some poetry; I should not be the only one having fun.

f) Reading books like this is a gift to yourself and others. Think dark chocolate; self awareness is rich stuff.

g) Don't give in to the negative doubts; you can do this.

Finally, know that you have not been alone in lying to yourself. Nearly everyone does it. The lie goes like this: "If I do not love like that again, I will not hurt that way again." It may be buried deep in the subconscious, but if you are wounded, this lie is probably there. The truth is, if you do not love again, you will hurt worse. If you are avoiding the idea of loving again, I suggest reading the following affirming paragraph outloud, ten times daily, for about three months. This will help you to correct your course, back to being and feeling alive.

"Restraining myself from loving is a violation to my heart, mind, and soul. I am created to love, and abandoning myself is even more painful than being abandoned by others. The grieving process can heal rejection and abandonment from others, and this process of healing requires that I love and accept myself so that I can feel whole again. So, today I will love and accept who I am, and I will be made whole again."

The statement "Today I will love and accept who I am, and I will be made whole again," is referred to as an affirmation. It is a road sign toward your personal and holy healing place. Just as you wouldn't yell at the sign that points to Pittsburgh and call it a liar because you are in New York, you do not tell affirmations they are wrong. They are just road signs -- pointing you in the direction that you must go in order to heal.

Furthermore, when you are ready, I invite you into the teal-blue waters of love, with full knowledge that these sun-filled days will pass sooner than you want them to pass. Swim anyway, strong with the muscles built from historic grieving, so that in the present moment of living, your life will be rich and full of truth-sharing intimacy. Or as my husband calls it, "in-to-me-see." There are always people to love; start with yourself.

Setbacks to harmony and serenity can be assumed. They will happen. Frequently, the loss of trust accompanies abrupt and terrible losses. Will you commit to never feeling that pain again, or will you learn to live with pain as an elementary part of loss? Your behaviors will reflect your commitment. Will you take steps to understand the way you personally grieve? Will you learn to let go, to flow with life, or will you shut down and back off from living and loving?

Many things can happen to hold you into the valley where you may lose sight of the mountain top. The trees can block out the hillside and the sunshine until that fateful winter comes. Then on a bleak and gray day, you see a mountain top you have never tried to reach before. During what may be your greatest trial, you may find your most surprising vision and strength.

Valleys and mountaintops are not always your choice; you are where you are. Under some circumstances you may have no alternative but to tolerate grief ripping through your body, a storm with a devastating path, and then later, rebuild. If there is a preparation time for planning death's visit, try to use it wisely.

Unfortunately, many of us forego this opportunity to get to know death (and our reactions to loss) for the experience of waiting for death to shake a fist in our faces, or drop us abruptly to our knees.

Ignoring and avoiding death as we do, it seems to be on a schedule beyond our control, with a life and mind of its own. If you will get to know death and loss, and the grieving process, and stay truthful as a healthy prevention of pain, then when death comes -- harshly or softly -- you will feel more prepared for the meeting.

my big, gray buddy

Grief - the kind mist, the torrential rain
grief - the storm ravaged pain
grief in the calm after the storm
remembering the good,
now accompanied by mourn
and a lack of trust for the new day born.
Neutralizing good with gone,
grief is a constant gray sky
grief - feelings of warmth and joy,
trumped by having to die
grief, my companion, my friend --
because I must love,
I will see you again.

kAh

SEVEN

Family

We took turns staying with Mom through the night during her last week. We had plenty of family willing to share in meeting Mom's needs. Each of us grieved our own way as she slept. We napped, we prayed, we remembered. During one of these nightly vigils, my brother reported he was thinking of friends and family members who had died, when suddenly the room filled up with a sense of their presence.

In her groggy state, Mom looked up, seemed to notice someone, and mumbled something about all those people in the room. She mentioned that dad was there, "Just waiting, I guess." My brother asked her a question about what she was seeing. Intellectualizing, Mom's mind snapped back, "I don't believe in that nonsense," and she went back to sleep.

To my brother, however, this was a holy moment. He said, "I felt something different in the room." Staying open to the process of living into dying allows for many such holy moments.

The nurses requested we leave the windows ajar, "to let the angels come for the person who is dying." We left them open for the angels, and for the balmy Colorado, September evenings, that sent a continuous, gentle, fresh breeze into the vanilla and death-scented room. I don't know what we would have done, had Mom died on a cold day in December. So many things seemed to come together when and how we needed them, even down to the week and the day.

My brother's birthday came on September 4th, and the morning meditation was titled "God's in Control of the Timing." I was grateful when Mom didn't die that day.

On September 5th, the morning meditation was titled "Coming Home." The scripture we read to Mom from Revelations described heaven. Mom listened and said, "That might be the first time I've enjoyed hearing Revelations."

Later that day, we asked if she wanted to hear it again, and she said, "No, once was enough." September 5th, the anniversary of Dad's death 35 years earlier, went slowly and quietly away...as did my mother, in the dark, early morning hour of 3 a.m. on September 6th.

Four of us were with mother in the room the morning she died. Not intentionally, but not surprisingly either, we represented: a) a biological child, b) a grandchild, c) a step-child, and d) a son in-law. Like the legs of a solid four-poster bed, the structure of our family had been squarely supporting mother. We took turns assisting her nurse in attention to her needs, which were becoming fewer and fewer. We listened to the shallow whispers of her breathing. We did not talk. We napped a little ourselves. We watched her arms reach into space as if swimming through a sleep tunnel into her next adventure. We waited in support for whatever would be her final efforts.

At a point when she was restless, I swept her child-like torso into my arms and rocked her. It was then that I whispered, "Bye-bye," and she returned my whisper with her own distant one, "Bye-bye." At the sound of her voice, my tears dripped into her wild, gray hair, and we spoke the second and third verses of this death song. "Bye-bye." "Bye-bye."

After a little more rocking, I laid her shoulders back down on the bed. She appeared so translucent and small. When she began to choke, I rolled her to her side. She stopped and seemed to sleep again. I left the room then, to walk the hall and treasure the holy moment quietly hand-in-hand with my daughter. While we were out, she died.

When we returned, my husband was at her head, and my step-brother looking on from across the bed. My husband tells it this way: "She didn't speak, but her eyes were looking at me as if to ask me how much longer. So I answered her, 'Well, Betty, your arms and legs are cold, and the signs of death have come up them now, and your face is beginning to look the way people look when you see them in a casket. It probably won't be long now, maybe an hour or two.' And then within two minutes, she died."

It was finished. Her mind shut down a system already vacated by the Spirit, and her body, left to itself, could not maintain life. Afterward, the room, still filled with respect for the remarkable dignity, grace, and intelligence she lived into her dying, became the scene of nurses and staff bringing closure for themselves and our holy moment with a few quietly read scriptures. From there, the family supported each other as we began to let the outside world know Mom had died.

Staying Together

We wondered, "Without Mom, how will we stay together as a family?" We are a complicated and amalgamated group. A bit with tongue in cheek, I have listed the briefest possible, factual outline. It is all true.

My father died when I was 21, and my brother was 23. We were both married, and I had one son. Six years later, Mother married a widower, who was also the minister of her church. He had a son and daughter. The son was married. The daughter was not. All three children who were married had children (by this time) from these marriages, bringing the grandchild count to 5 boys and 2 girls.

Over the years, all three marriages dissolved, and all three remarried. The minister's daughter also married, and had two boys, and then two more boys, from the minister's son's second marriage, brought the grandchild count to 9 boys and 2 girls. The remarriages brought children from previous marriages into the scene, including 3 more boys and one more girl. So the grandchildren numbered 12 boys and 3 girls. Three of the grandchildren brought 3 great-grandchildren, all boys. Whew!

So Mom's children, counting married spouses, numbered 8, along with 3 former spouses, who are parents to some of the grandchildren, numbering 15, and 3 great grandchildren.

There will be no test on this, for you anyway. Mom helping this family to accept and to love each other was no small feat. Now the minister's daughter's sons never knew another "grandmother," than my mother. All the grandchildren called her Baba. Neither the mix, nor the blend mattered. The importance of mother in each person's life, regardless of bloodline was all we needed to understand.

Additional intimate facts: My first husband's second wife came with tears in her eyes to Mom's funeral. My brother's first spouse also came respectfully. Jerre Tjardes sang equally beautifully at the minister's funeral (1994), his wife's funeral (1973), and Mom's funeral (2003). She did her student teaching in music in my elementary school. I have been blessed by knowing this musical woman since I was in the sixth grade.

The continuity of Mom's community were like soft cushions upon which to lean. The familiar faces of the Baseys, the Harberts, Marie, Louella, and dozens more came to honor Betty and comfort her family. I felt safely surrounded.

Three weeks later, I went back to her church's 100 year anniversary, and I sat in "her pew." Her best friend sat down beside me. I wept from fresh grief at her absence, openly within her loving church family.

Sharing Mom's Things

Mom had collections of figurines, to include some pretty dishes, ceramic bells, Ylladro from Spain, Hummels from Germany, and Christmas items from around the world.

The undesignated items (or so I thought) were combined on a window bench. I thought Mom's neighbors and the people who worked at Bonnel, including some of her nurses, would like to have one of the "leftover" figurines as a keepsake. So, I gave out the word, via one of the friendlier cleaning ladies. The second person to come was a shy, small hispanic person from some area of Bonnel, maybe the kitchen, I'm not certain. She looked over the items on the window bench and picked out an old, valuable Hummel.

I'm fairly certain I looked surprised, but all I said to her was. "You have very good taste. That is a very special one. I hope you enjoy it, and take good care of it."

"Oh, yes," she said. "I will." And she and the Hummel left.

After she was gone, I looked through the items and picked out the rest of the Hummels that I had missed keeping for the family. Later we laughed together, and decided Mom would have laughed with us, and enjoyed my extended bonus to this sweet person, whoever she was.

Principles

A few years prior to their church celebrating this 100 year anniversary, some members began gathering the complete, available information about the history of the church. They wrote a substantial memoir for the 100-year celebration. They tell me no one is mentioned more in the book than my mother. At this 100 year anniversary, Mother's 75 year membership was honored posthumously.

I think it is worth taking a moment to consider the principles mother seemed to live by, the by-product of which was a strong family unit, respect from her community, and a long, productive life. She lived well, despite hardships, and she died well into her routine of living. The following is a list, as I see it, of some of the truly dignified, loving, and faith filled principles that mother characteristically exemplified.

1. She remained true to herself, her belief in God, and her lifetime goal of helping others.

2. She generously gave of her resources, especially her high intelligence, her time, and her money.

3. She used her high intelligence in gentle ways, so that others seldom felt less intelligent.

4. She kept her focus on what she felt called to do, both vocationally, and personally.

5. Even when she believed she was right, she agreed to disagree amicably.

6. Even when she knew she was wrong, she insisted on agreeing to disagree amicably. (Numbers 5 and 6 meant we were going to stay connected, no matter what.)

7. She repeatedly adapted well to change, with as little bitterness and resentment as possible, and seldom with judgment.

8. She lived in a way that she would have few regrets when the time came to reveal them.

9. She was appreciative, and she showed it.

10. She continued to question and ponder the profound things in life. She took an interest in current affairs and politics.

11. She held others in high regard.

12. She brought dignity to every situation.

I do pray, "God grant me the ability to walk my path as graciously as Mother walked hers."

Our family has not remained as close as when mom was alive, but we have maintained the definition of being "family." I cannot imagine being family without any of them. I believe they feel similarly, but we live in different states, focusing on our children in the different stages of their lives. We have made stronger efforts than before, when we relied on Mom to bring us together for a reason. We continue on a learning curve which she rounded years ahead of us. Maybe that curve is partially a generational difference.

I am so grateful for the preparation we did have; it helped to make our transition smoother. She paved the way for us to be with her -- and to be without her.

Savannah Elizabeth

One special event has happened that seems to have touched all our hearts, and seems especially significant to my brother and myself. My granddaughter was born on September 5th, 2004. At 5 a.m., as I headed to the hospital to be with my daughter and her husband in the delivery of their baby, I knew the day was the anniversary of Dad's death. On this date for the past 36 years, I had remembered arriving home in the dark hours of early morning, to a hug from my brother in an Army uniform. Choosing to let go, into a new direction, I decided this September 5th, the birth of a new life, was the perfect day for this change. Savannah Elizabeth (named after Mom) claimed this day for her birth.

"She gets the next 36 years, just in case I live that long," I told my daughter, after she remembered the historic relevance of the date.

Finally, a tiny baby, with the ease of tossing a coin, transformed the last residual of my grief to joy. I cannot think of a greater symbol of creation than new life. September 5th is now my grandchild's birthday, and when I called my brother, he shared in my joy.

A Post Script: Currently, Savannah is just one week short of a year old. Yesterday, at my office, she found a box full of magazines, that she carefully sorted. Standing only a few inches higher than the box, she leaned over, picked up a magazine, looked at it, and threw it on the floor at her feet. I couldn't help but laugh, and remember how much Mom enjoyed her work, which at times included weeding out old books from the shelves, she happily "pitched."

Family is the handprint of passing on things we see and things we do not see.

If you are using this book as part of a study or support group, I invite you to write the principles by which you live. How are you preparing yourself for such major changes in your life as growing older, simplifying your life, and eventually dying? You may want to compare your principles to the ones I have listed in this chapter. You could look up Bible verses, or consider laws and ethical standards, and how they help to guide you to choose principles by which you live. There may be some principles that have been "handed down" to you by parents and teachers. Family "scripts" are widely varied, and not always positive. Examples might be, "don't trust people whose last names end in "ez" or "people who aren't Christian are bad." Negative scripts prevail in dysfunctional families.

"Don't trust your sister," or "always take care of your brother," would be family scripts that might have originated from either abusive *or* loving situations. Identifying the family scripts you really want to keep can be extra clarifying. Without consciously identifying them, many of them stay hidden from view, but intact, like a brake that won't release. Negative ones echo the confused feelings of "I'm not enough."

Stronger than scripts, well-chosen principles are supported by healthy communities over time. They are rich ideas gifted to us through the wisdom of those who have gone before us. They are not permanent, but rather cured.

EIGHT

Preparation

We plan goals for life. Why not plan for a peaceful death as part of that life? If you have a knowledge that you are safe, you will prepare helpful instructions for others. If you have a knowledge that you are provided for, you will provide for others. If you have a knowledge that you are loved, you will take away as much of the pain as possible from the loss your death will bring, not by being secretive or obtuse, but by sharing the truth in a caring way, as this truth is needed.

When I heard the change to weakness in my mother's voice, I packed and drove to Colorado. She had never sounded weak before. It was a 22 hour drive, one way. During the drive, I grieved, listened to my heart, and thought about the choices that I might have ahead of me. I knew my mother had made certain decisions that we had discussed, but truthfully, I felt uncertain about my readiness for mother to die. I was frightened for both of us.

The day after I arrived, Mom and I were sitting together in the Physical Therapy Room, waiting for her therapist. She said, "You didn't think it would happen this way, did you?"

Surprised a little by her bluntness, I responded, "No."

Looking at Mother in her wheelchair, she wasn't the strong woman I was used to. I couldn't hold back the tears, and I tried to match her honesty with blunt humor. "You were supposed to drop dead of a heart attack, remember?"

We were laughing and crying when the Occupational Therapist arrived to hook Mom up to a bicycle, but then changed her mind.

She explained. "We are in a difficult place. We want to do things to strengthen your heart, and support your muscles, but we don't want to set you back with too much work." (It was that paradox thing that happens as we age.)

I was instructed to hold a pole, that Mom tried pulling herself up on from her wheelchair. She was proud of herself after several strong efforts. "I'm tired, but it's a good tired," she said, meaning, "I've worked hard." We agreed with her.

Then we tossed a beach ball back and forth between us. In 55 years, I had never played ball with my mother. I would never have planned that either: *Line item 49,757a: Toss a beach ball seven days before mother dies.* We actually laughed and had fun, much the way I would with my grandchild. It was a bright colored, plastic ball as round as a stearing wheel, that she worked hard to catch and throw back to me. Why does that fill up such an empty place just thinking about it now? Who could have ever guessed!

So, when I talk about planning to die in your life, part of the plan is to accept and enjoy whatever you can in the process of living, as you step into the dying. It might be watching a movie together, playing checkers, singing a song, or listening to the birds.

I picked fresh raspberries from the plants in the nursing home's courtyard and brought them to Mother. I don't know if they were sprayed or bad for us. In my memory now, as they did then, they taste sweet and perfect. We didn't have to mention the great raspberries Dad grew when I was growing up; we knew we both remembered. It was a mutually serendipitous and sweet moment. We also both knew she was very ill, and probably dying. Maybe it made the pilfered raspberries even more delightful.

My brother brought his homemade soup, fresh bread and late summer watermelon. He lovingly helped Mom feed herself. It was a picnic, just one week before she died. The cool Colorado evening, my sister-in-law's soft voice, my brother's tenderness all set the stage for my mother's last full supper. No one could have planned a better doorway into her final stage of living. With only a little hesitance, we accepted the stepping up to it.

During the last week, frequently a soft, short sigh rippled from Mother's mouth. It was the kind that follows deep sobbing, only my mother was not outwardly crying. This was one of many signs, not only of her coming death, but also the style in which she was going to die. She seldom complained in life; nor did she complain in her dying.

Death is the timing of the Plan of the Universe meeting with the Human Plan. As we saw the merging of these plans, Mother's choices appeared remarkably wise. There is no shot or pill for openness and wisdom, two of the most essential ingredients for being prepared for life. Furthermore, mental, emotional, and physical health seem prerequisite to being open and wise. So is this another question of the chicken or the egg coming first? Do only open and wise people become healthy? Is there a gene or a predisposition toward wisdom, curiosity, and the capacity and interest in learning?

For example, why are you reading this book? Are you reading in memory of Betty because you knew her? Is it to prepare yourself for dealing with death more effectively? Have you been offered this book because you are already deep into your grief? Is someone you love dying? Are you reading with an open mind toward making death the final and honorable part of your living?

Without preparation, death is like a required meal, for which you have no groceries. If sudden, you take what is on the pantry shelf -- okay -- pork and beans, green beans, and sauerkraut. That's hardly palatable, let alone appetizing. Many deaths do come quickly. My mother knew. So, she loaded up her pantry early, for just such an occasion as her own death.

She and my step-father always had current wills, that named each other beneficiaries, until my step-father required twenty-four hour nursing care due to his condition of Parkinson's Disease with dementia. Then Mother rewrote her will, and let us all know about it. We did not need that new document for nine years, but I am certain it brought her peace of mind to know her will was up-to-date. Equally important, her estate was simple to settle, thanks to the will, and other clearly outlined documents. Her preparation of our family modeled for us the courtesy of her openness and wisdom.

No stranger to the effects of old age on the body, mind, and spirit (she lived at a nursing home), Mom would remind us, "as people get older, their lifelong faults become exaggerated." It was such a concern to her that she worked very hard to become less flawed, so that she wouldn't become more concentrated in them instead.

The one area she missed, was in her openness (early

enough) to alternative healing, such as chiropractic and massage. Regular massages (like the regularity of her hair appointments) might have cut back on the stress she carried that translated into problems with her heart, and pain in her legs and back. Early chiropractic might have straightened her uneven hips so that her back pain was not so severe in her last few years. The accupuncturist she finally saw told her she came to him too late. He didn't believe his treatment would help by the time she decided to try this alternative.

It was one of the few areas in which Mom demonstrated some rigidity. She wouldn't veer far from her comfort zone, which was deeply entrenched in western medicine. The more experiences that I had to the contrary, the more she felt the need to defend her doctors. She didn't trust her own intuition until she was dying, and I had not trusted her doctors until they told me the truth of the paradoxical effect of her heart medicines. Despite such stubborness in each of us, we found a balance in the end, but in our stronger years of disagreeing, the harder she shut down against alternative health care, the more I wanted to be a part of it. The more mystical I became, the deeper she planted herself in western medicine. Eventually, I stopped worrying about her crooked gait, and she stopped telling me about her aches and pains, that is, until she began dying.

As we both aged, we saw little value in arguing, so we agreed to disagree and be friends, despite our differences. These became the best years of our lives with each other. We traveled together; went on cruises, planned our vacations with other family members, and generally enjoyed each other.

I did worry briefly about her one time in Seattle. Our

cruise ship stopped over, and we decided to take a walk. We got caught in a downpour of rain without an umbrella. Taking as much of a short cut as possible, with no taxis in sight, we giggled and dragged each other as quickly as our old legs would go through the puddles, literally, to our port in the storm. Taking time to change would mean missing lunch, so we sat with strangers, pretending we always looked like "drowned rats," as Mom put it.

Gratefully, we both understood what a miracle it really was that she hadn't had an angina attack, or worse yet a heart attack, on the way back to the ship. "Thank God you didn't die that day," I would tease her, and she would add, "I thought about it." She did think enough about her death that she created many circumstances that helped to make her departure orderly, financially sound, and well-defined.

Openness is essential;
secrecy does not need to be a secondary sledge hammer
to a family in pain and in shock.

Mom became involved with the nursing home in which my step-father resided until his death. She was active on the board and committees. Bonell Good Samaritan Nursing Home created a remarkable model of step-down care, before the new clinical vernacular, *palliative care*. This is care for the dying in their final phase of living, which might embrace years, not just months. Mother respected Bonell's central theme of respect and kindness toward patients, and the level of care that covered a broad spectrum of need in a person's final years.

She chose to move into a new apartment complex

located on the nursing home grounds when she was 80. At this age, she was capable of staying in her condominium, but she saw the benefit (even beyond what we could see for her) of living at Bonell. Her cronies tried to discourage her. "Why are you moving into a nursing home; you don't need that!" they told her.

Through a sequence of choices, she brought us her gift of wisdom. Mother wanted to live in the "new, beautiful apartments." She would have her independence, a place to park her car, a community of older people, and lunch cooked for her everyday. She appreciated this vision for herself, but it was, of course, more expensive than living in her condominium. She figured what she would make selling the condo, and how much money she would need to use from the investment of the profit. She had to be able to add just enough to her personal pension plan, the small benefit from my step-father's pension, and her monthly social security.

She ran these figures by me after she had done the math, but only for communication. She was, of course, accurate in her planning. She sold the condominium, made about what she thought she would make, and we had the amount she believed we would have to split up when it was all over. That is remarkable insight, planning, and sharing. What if all 80 year olds handled themselves and their finances so wisely?

Our Bonus

Mom added a bonus of free, indoor, family "garage sales." She would clean out cupboards and closets, and pile things on cardtables. She filled the tables with things she knew she would not use in her apartment life at Bonell.

Then she would invite the family over to Sunday dinner, and to flea marketing in the living room afterwards. We all had fun hauling boxes of things home after dinner. There was never an exchange of money. If it was on a table, she no longer wanted it.

"Ann, don't you need one of these? No, I thought of you when I saw it." We laughed and we ribbed Mom about her catalog shopping. "I already got one of these for Christmas; do we all have one of these?" "Maybe," she'd laugh back. We shared in the fun over dividing up the spoils. We left more than half on the tables, which Mother sent to a local women's shelter the next day.

Mom had a lot of slides, photos, and momentos of trips. She did her best to narrow it down, but we still have a few boxes full. She did carefully share historic, family photos from generations back, with as many explanations as she could remember. She was good about throwing away ones that didn't mean anything, and disgarding the papers and cards that can drive a family crazy when the last of a generation passes.

She prepared us by making priorities about her things. She prepared us by living more simply as she grew older. She showed us it was okay to need less. She prepared us by making decisions early and easily.

We heard, "Oh, your father gave me that for..." or "I think mother had that made for...." or "Uncle Pete and Aunt Mary gave me that when...," so we gained reasons for keeping or not keeping things.

The more informed we became about her things, the more we learned about her life. These times became our baby steps toward our grief work, without our even knowing.

Whether circumstantial or divine inspiration, it worked well. We had fun together. We sorted and divided a lot of her stuff. She threw out things with little meaning, while moving gently toward the simpler life. All this happened as a result of Mom's choice to move to an apartment when she could have still managed in her condominium.

Shifting downward into a simpler life will feel like either gain or loss. Unresolved losses push aside the idea of empowerment, as grief accumulates with grief from other losses. Empowerment to live more simply happens when the losses from the past are mostly resolved.

Unresolved losses (regard the Loss Time Line you began in Chapter One) can burden the heart and soul so much, that anything "less than" can only be seen as another loss. Mom had worked hard on her own grief issues when her second husband passed. She discovered then about the accumulation effect grief has. She chose to work through grief she felt for the loss of my dad and my step-dad by attending a program called *Windows* (sold by Active Parenting out of Marietta, Georgia) offered at the time by her church.

So, when Mother felt the time had come to simplify her life, she was empowered, and actually enjoyed taking charge of the simplification. Mother believed the way a person ends their life, if they have any say about that ending, reflects the way they lived it. As always, she invited the entire family to participate with her whenever she made a shift into simpler living.

For example, once it was the topic of spending less on our birthdays. Then she began to spend less on Christmas. She traveled less often, so there were no more gifts from trips. When she moved to Bonell, she stopped entertaining the family. We entertained her more often instead.

None of these shifts into simpler living meant that she loved us less. We didn't take it that way. In fact, we felt more valued than ever by this loving woman whose world was closing, while our worlds were opening, because she made known her intention of staying connected.

If a person has been distant, isolated, moody, selfish, fearful, or bitter, there is a good chance they will die that way. Fortunately for us, Mother had been generous, curious, interested in books and places, friendly, and believed, generally, in the goodness of people.

She probably had more clothes and catalogs than she needed, but not at the expense of many small attentions to each member of the family, nor to her larger generous donations to charities and her church. She was always ready to listen to our latest escapades. She did her best to share in our lives without being invasive. We all liked her and we all miss her. She helped us to have special memories and tokens representing her life, well before she became an old, sick person. Ultimately, knowing her was our finest preparation.

The Will

Ownership is elementary. A will covers this topic, and is essential for settling the estate smoothly after someone dies. One must have a will before dying; you cannot write it afterwards. (Don't laugh, unless you just can't help it.)

I believe the vast majority of people who put off having a will are arrogant or superstitious. Arrogance thinks: "I'm not going to die, why write a will!" Superstition says: "If I write my will, then I will die." Writing a will doesn't bring about dying, and thinking it will never happen doesn't keep it away.

True, life is complicated, so we find reasons for putting off such practical things as writing our wills. We've changed names, adopted a child, moved our accounts, have used up the savings, have complex financial arrangements with the mother-in-law, etc.

Don't allow your excuse to be, "I can't afford an attorney." Several quick and easy sources exist. Online, legalzoom.com, will create a will for you for $59. There is no attorney; you represent yourself. If this will is contested, however, California becomes the jurisdiction for the contest. Always read the agreement that comes with any online contract.

Pre-paid Legal is a service that has an annual fee, but will cover many (simple) questions at no additional cost, and they will help you to create a legal will. They use local attorneys, but can also be initialized online.

1StopLegal.com offers many choices, by state, for downloading legal forms. They range in cost from $12-$80 for a will. Some local attorneys will probably document your will for $80 if you ask them ahead for a special fee.

As I was researching resources for Caregivers, I came across a great workbook published by Caring Resources in Nashville, TN. The publication is titled *Help! Where Are All My Papers? A practical guide to identify and organize "must know" information.*

One notebook they sell has special Caregiver Information included, and a second one is for regular folks. Either can be ordered through www.caringresources.com. Sample forms are included, which moves you toward a finish line. By filling in some blanks, you are beginning the process of becoming organized.

Another resource for planning is *Long-Term Care; Your Financial Planning Guide* by Phyllis Shelton (Kensington Books, 2003). Commit to yourself and your loved ones to read this and make a plan.

Nearly anything you would do, in good conscience, with a witness (or even better, notorization by a notary public -- check your bank) is probably going to be better than nothing.

A will is essential in order to avoid a great expenditure of time and energy (to say nothing of the possible legal mess) at a time when you will continue, like it or not, with your grieving. Furthermore, a power-of-attorney may be important under some medical conditions, and please have your desires in print about what to do about your body and the end of your life. Consider the circumstance of not having a voice (or a mind) to share your opinion, and make known your preferences. Describe appropriate circumstances for pulling the plug on your life. Don't just moan and groan about the awful things others experience. Put your concerns and wishes in writing.

Appointing a representative or an executor (different terms for different states) is the decision of the person dying. If they don't make this decision, the court may likely become the executor of your loved one's estate. There is always an estate, regardless of the size. If your loved one is dying, and he or she does not have a will, an estate attorney needs to be called into the situation, with as much respect and dignity for the person who is passing. The person dying needs to decide beneficiaries, and a representative for their estate, after they pass. They also need to list and locate assets, annuities, and important papers. There may be directives about carrying out certain wishes. Not all of your desires may happen after you die, but even fewer will happen if they are not connected legally to your assets, through a Last Will and Testament. **A will does not need to be complicated; it just needs to be.** Because you don't know **when** it needs to be, do it now.

Organization

Organized persons will have these discussions way ahead of the time of dying. Mother had already informed her children where the important papers were located, and everything that was in the will was known ahead of time. I was on her bank account, and had been for years, so it was easy to draw out money to take care of expenses. While legally, that money was not inherited because it "belonged" to me, I treated it as money that belonged to all of us, and accounted fully for it to my siblings. I simply used it, and a portion of the inheritance to pay the bills, and then divided up what was left four ways, just as mother wanted.

Mother already had her burial plot purchased and paid for, so her burial cost (her) one fifth what we would have paid for it had we had to purchase it at the time of her death. Her funeral service was also arranged and paid for. The one thing they billed us was $900 for taking the dirt in and out of the hole in which she was buried. (It felt like a "gotcha," because, well, have you tried to bury someone without removing the dirt?) Finally, she had left the tombstone (matching my father's) for us to pay, which of course, we were honored to do.

Someone else in the family had an extra key to the safety deposit box, as part of the distribution of responsibilities. I don't believe anyone felt overwhelmed by logistics, thanks to Mom. Maybe part of the reason Mom was so prepared was because of her history of a heart surgery, a hysterectomy, and two (angioplasty) heart procedures. We just called them all "surgery." And we waited in the waiting room nervously, quietly, faithfully, and together, her family. Each time, we wondered if she would surface, and each time she did. I remember wondering once if she was invincible, but of course I knew better. I knew she would die someday, but concern about her paperwork was never an extra burden.

In the area of paperwork, Mother was the adult, leading her adult children. She was more realistic, older and wiser. It is wonderful when the parent can lead, and the children can follow. Not all parents do this, and many adult children find themselves frustrated with the level of immaturity with which their parents handle the necessary preparations toward their final years and days.

Stepping Down

When mother needed to step down from her condominium, she had already moved into an apartment. When she needed to step down from her apartment, she was already part of a nursing home in which she could move within familiar spaces to receive extended medical treatment. When she no longer needed medical treatment, they were prepared for her to need extended nursing care. In addition to the extended nursing care, they suggested we consider inviting hospice. Because we have trained therapists in the family, we didn't feel the need for hospice, but we were glad for the offer. When our information base depleted, the nurses and staff supported us. When she died, they called the funeral home with whom Mom had made arrangements to come get her body. After her death, her papers were found to be in order; her bills were paid, and over the next six months, her estate was settled simply, and legally.

Everything that happened was made easier by preparation and organization. That is eleven or more events where many families feel extra pain when difficulties and unpredictable things occur. In the situation of Mother's death, the preparation and organization unfolded smoothly, and continued with blessings into our daily lives for months after her death.

The more prolonged a person's dying, certainly the more things can go wrong, but also the more opportunity the family has to become unified.

Consider the possibility that a dying person may not feel they *can* leave until the family becomes more united about his or her death! What a bind we may put people in who are needing or wanting to die, by not being more personally prepared for the truth of their death. I understand not wanting to believe that someone is dying, and toward the end, they often rally. This causes confusion, since nearly every dying person rallies a few hours or days before they actually die.

Knowing ahead of time may help you to take advantage of this clarity when it happens. Communicate, enjoy being close, and prepare each other with honor and dignity around the truth of the situation. Denial, if still engaged, will try to make this brief lucidity one more shred of hope in a belief that your loved one is really not dying.

Even if this clarity lasts much longer than expected, use it to build intimacy, truth sharing, enjoyment and laughter together, final wonderful moments, rather than pumping up false expectations.

I believe that mother's death was largely connected to her living beliefs. She thrived on life. Post thirty years as a professional librarian, Mother retired to enjoy volunteering, reading, traveling, church, activities with friends and families, concerts and plays, and creating charts of geneology. She considered this living. As she could do less and less, she became less interested in living. This seems a normal progression to me, especially for someone who has experienced as rich and full a life as she had.

In this way, her life prepared her for living with ease into death. Those who have had abbreviated lives, histories of unresolved trauma, and little personal satisfaction, seem to have much more difficulty in "learning to let go now," to use Mother's phrase.

Unfair and Cheated

Perhaps the greatest barrier to letting go, is the lack of preparation for the unfairness of life. We feel cheated if a child dies, or becomes too ill to enjoy life. We are often confused and frustrated by the presence of disabilities. There is no way to feel prepared for having an adult child suddenly in a coma, or living on machines, dying in a war, or suddenly being disabled for life. Regardless of fair or unfair circumstances, knowing more about death (and the path it may take), may help us to let go when we need to, of either large primary losses, or the many secondary ripples that we experience off the primary losses.

I know something of walking the high wire between hoping the best for my child, and truthfully realizing his handicapping conditions. I have a thirty-five year old disabled son. He is mentally retarded, speech-impaired, and was born without ears. He hears, aided by a bone conductor. I am fiercely protective of this person, and at the same time, I've had to back down hundreds of times and let him decide his own destiny, in order to allow his continued, albeit slow, growth toward independence. It's a high wire I'm used to walking by now, but I don't believe that I could say my motions through life with this young man ever felt prepared.

I remember cartoon characters who, while trying to survive a terribly strong wind, would grab a tree, and wave in the wind like a flag with their legs perpendicular to the tree. This is the difficult, vulnerable posture that comes to my mind when I think of these years with my son's disabilities.

If I am to see life as something with order to it, then lessons generated in confusion have to fit somewhere into a larger picture. Any one part of my life must fit reasonably well with other parts. Perhaps I have used my ability to fly (perpendicular with my legs off the ground) in parenting, in teaching, and in counseling. Maybe I also used this when Momma was dying.

In the west, we call it "taking the steer by the horns." That's rodeo lingo, I think, since during roping exercises, the cowboy leans over, jumps from his horse on top of a young steer, wrestles it to the ground by twisting his neck by the horns, until the steer loses his balance (and gets three legs tied into a rope) or the cowboy loses his steer. The parallel to unfair, is that tragedies often wrestle us to our knees, tying us up with circumstances beyond our control. Sometimes we even get branded in the process!

The roping exercise is preparation for branding season, but probably we all would prefer to be the cowboy rather than the steer. Having grown up in the west, and literally out of pioneer stock, I guess the thought has been passed down to me, "Somebody has to do it, it might as well be you; you take the steer by the horns."

Mother knew this part of who I am. She knew that if I could, I would take care of her, up until the very end. Unfairly, life had prepared me for her dying. In fairness to herself and her family, however, she had prepared for herself to die.

Frankly, her preparation and organization contributed to a much needed balance in my life, between fair and unfair. So much about her final days on earth soaked into my sponge-like psyche. Building a family that could trust and rely on each other encouraged us all to forge ahead, even when we knew death was imminent. Despite the tragic and unfair times in our lives, the balance of fairness arrived.

I believe this happened because we were a community that understood the pain of loss and grief, *and* the need to willingly risk loving again despite the history of losses.

Open sharing of truth is not the same thing as "wallowing" in pain. I am not an advocate of complaining or whining. Neither do I think that hiding the truth, avoiding the painful truth, or keeping secrets really helps in the long run. Gentle sharing and caring comes inside of balance. The key is ENOUGH.

While each situation is unique, generally speaking, not telling someone the truth will not save them from the difficult feelings. Furthermore, the postponement of telling the truth may regrettably defer the intimate sharing... forever.

The Difficult, Intimate Journey

I remember the first time Mom called me to ask me to come take her to the hospital. I lived in a town thirty minutes away from her. It was a Saturday morning in the Spring of 1989. My step father still lived at home, despite serious dementia. Mom said he would be okay, and she had called his daughter to come stay with him. Meanwhile, she and I went to the emergency room. I had no idea until that morning how sick Mom really was. She probably didn't either, but she was wise to respond to a pain that was more than her customary pains of angina.

She was admitted of course, after doctors decided she had had a mild heart attack. Within two days, she was having four-way bypass heart surgery that was going to require several weeks of recovery, during which time she would be unable to care for my step father.

We siblings met together to discuss the complication Mother's health dilemma presented to her caregiving position at home. We organized into teams, one for Mom and one for Les, her husband, with my brother and my step sister heading the team in charge of researching our alternatives for caring for Les. Unprepared as we were, we needed to find more truth before we could find answers. We prepared ourselves by listening and sharing (dialoguing is different than just talking). With empathy and caring, we worked together toward clear insights and understandings.

This was the turning point for relieving mother of

care taking duties we believed she was no longer capable of managing. Her heart disease moved her beyond being able to manage life with Les at home. This was when we discovered Bonell and their excellent step-downs available for the elderly. Les went to a new home, and Mother came home to an empty one.

There is nothing fair about diseases that erase the mind and its awareness of someone you love. Les had pastored many people during a long career of ministry, but it was hard for many of them to come see him. As soon as Mom could, she visited him daily, but toward the end, she was often his only visitor. How many times do you come back, when the person you are visiting doesn't know your name?

One thing I found delightful and amazing about Les, even at the height of his dementia, was his ability to recite scriptures. He had officiated so many weddings and funerals that I only had to begin a verse, and he would smile and finish the scripture with a lilt. Then he would return to reporting a thirty year old memory as if it had happened that day to him.

Mother was a successful spouse to two men who left her. That had to contribute to her heart problems, as did the genes from her father, who died of a heart attack at my feet one day. I sang at his funeral, "I Walked Today Where Jesus Walked," which ends, "and felt him (Jesus) close to me." A couple of decades later, I sang the song somewhere simply to know that I could. Then I retired the piece. It was an emotionally difficult solo for me. However, it must have meant a great deal to Mother, for when we spoke about the music at her funeral she looked briefly ever-so-hopeful toward me. "I can't," I said. And she said, "Of course not."

Knowing and expressing our limitations is so very important in the prevention of extra pain and guilt. While I would have loved to have told mother I would sing for her, one last time, I would have to have said it in truth, not just what I would wish I could do. Feeling sad now, that I could not do this is much better I think than feeling the guilt I would feel if I had told her I could do something that I could not make happen, or that I would have done poorly.

As it is said, "the road to hell is paved with good (but unfounded and unrealistic) intentions." The long and intimately caring road is paved with provision, preparation, flexible acceptance of fair and unfair, and integrity.

Failure to prepare for your desires to be known will result in confusion, and possibly legal complications. Provide a path of your choice, as best as you can. Incorrectly or prematurely going off track can happen instantly, through unexpected circumstances. There are no guarantees, I know, but as little confusion as possible is all right to hope and plan.

Death is neither the time nor the place to expect clarity to accidentally show up. That is why death, and all its ramifications, should be discussed, if possible, while you are still fully participating in your life. This discussion may provide hope, calm some of your fears, and allow an early relief valve in the grieving process.

If you and your loved ones haven't yet begun true preparations, perhaps you can begin now. It is not so much the planning of the when, or even the how of your dying. It is the planning of addressing the idea, today, of your dying someday.

Living is a dance. Death is the stepping into the final movements of this dance. It is okay to hope for a song you can sing, and a dance you can dance. Pray for that. Plan for that. If your experience falls short of your hopes, your preparation will still help break the fall. There will be fewer consequences and less to fear for those who make some effort to prepare.

Sprinkled throughout the years, it is small amounts of life-balancing salt, rather than a truckload dumped at your front door as a surprise ending. Invest in some of the resources I've mentioned. Leave organized documentation, not short notes for a scavenger hunt.

Don't confuse being prepared with being in control. Preparation should be done from the place of caring for yourself, as well as caring about the loved ones you will leave behind. This is an honoring of the relationship, not about who is "in control." Getting your life in order is about being truthful about your own and other person's needs.

Just as Mother cleaned her closets and cupboards, offering us the opportunity to take what we needed, she as generously helped to meet the needs of others by charitable giving. If your lifetime with family members has proved unsatisfactory for some reason, attempts at revenge through your Final Will and Testament can only provide more fuel for future dissent. Consider a goal of harmony and unification in your Will. The true preparation, however, comes in the living, truth sharing, daily generosity, and the work of caring relationships within your friends and family.

Fight the urge to greet opportunities to discuss death with nervous suggestions to change topics.

Using dignity and respect, work hard to stay focused

on the real circumstances. When someone you care about is dying, it is a good time to focus on just being. Being there for a loved one. Being yourself. Being quiet. Being thoughtful. Being patient. Being kind. If you are not used to doing these things, read the rest of this book in preparation of yourself for your consideration of being.

Ambiguity

It is somewhat natural, I think, to find death both intriguing and repulsive. These opposing mindsets are too often oversimplified into a dichotomy. The chemistry of procreation draws us toward another, and the chemistry of protection draws us away. We often call the one love, and the other fear or avoidance. We sometimes escape into the escalation of the cycle of calm and arousal, by quickly pushing through times of calm so that we can once again feel stimulated by a crisis, a problem, a dilemma, or an unknown.

Throughout these chapters I have suggested that calm and serenity will lead to healing and satisfaction, even during disruptive moments or events in your life. If you have already worked to create these things in your life, you don't need instruction. You are prepared. If you have not worked to create harmony, peace, and serenity within your family community, you may not know the value of these things. How will you learn now?

Is the middle ground with the Big Gray Buddy somewhere between intrigue and repulsion? Or is serenity found in a place apart from the daily grind? You will identify your losses, with help if you need it; and you will begin to grieve your losses, with help if you need it. If you need help, there will be people near you who need to help others as part of their own need to grow and heal. The Order of the Universe is such that you will likely find each other for the season of growth...just as Edith found me when I needed her.

NINE

Grief-in-Limbo

We picked his name before he was born --William, after his father's grandfather, and Harold after my dad. My husband had felt close to his grandfather, and well, I still missed Dad terribly. I became pregnant with William fifteen months after Dad's death. William was to arrive in September, historically a happy month, filled with family birthdays and beautiful Fall days, including the newness and excitement of the first Autumn-crisp days of school. More recently, it was an ominous month, marred by the violent loss of my dad.

My pregnancy seemed normal.

At the time of William's birth, my husband was taking a graduate school break from his military career, studying thermal dynamics in Geophysics at the Colorado School of Mines, which was located close to Mom. Life was trying to rebalance. My 18 month old son's playfulness was pivotal. He was central to our attentions. He tumbled in and out of the shallow swimming pool in the yard, until his diaper would get so wet it would fall off.

Mom and I couldn't help but laugh at him, watching his charming playfulness. This provided hours of relief and joy from the grief we still carried. Viet Nam was looming for my husband, but temporarily he was safe at home, with me, our son, and another child on the way. A tiny light seemed to appear at the end of the tunnel. (You know -- that oncoming train.)

Because my previous labors were very short, we thought it best for me to be induced at the hospital. They broke my water, and the larger than normal amount served as a warning to the doctors that not all was well for William. Of course, they said nothing to me.

Extra doctors and nurses were in the room when I delivered. They held him up for me to see, and whisked him from the delivery room. He looked fine to me, and I felt happy on the gas I had inhaled for the pain, since my labor came too fast for a spinal block. About an hour or two later, a doctor and my husband came into the recovery area to tell me that William was born without ears, and with a cleft palate. In that moment, although I didn't know it, I began my grief-in-limbo.

Why? It is the only question at first. What would be the ramifications of not having ears? Was he deaf too? Could he eat? These questions would soon follow, but first there was only "Why has this happened? Why now? Why no ears? Why me, Lord?" I asked why all night long as I gazed out an enormous window into the dark sky, broken every few minutes by the headlights of airplanes landing at Denver's airport. The pin points of light would grow into recognizable head lights, and zoom over my head, leaving a dark sky behind. It's a fairly strong parallel to the waves of grief that would be a part of the perpetual, unknowable future.

Around 5 a.m. I felt hungry. I had missed having dinner the previous night, and I was tired of asking a question that I sensed (rightly so) would never have an answer.

I went in search of some food. After some cereal and milk, I walked to the nursery, went in, and asked to feed my baby. I had no idea how foolish the request appeared, in light of his handicap. William had no roof to his mouth. No one knew exactly how to feed him yet. My ignorance seemed to protect me, until a nurse said, "Can you do that?"

I must have looked at her as if she were crazy.

"He's my son, who else will feed him?"

"He has a cleft palate. He cannot suck," said one nurse.

"Well, do you have a bottle or something? How have *you* been feeding him?"

With some awkwardness, I am realizing now, they glanced at several kinds of bottles in his make-shift layette, and handed one, along with William, into my arms. I am quessing that they did not have an idea of what to do with me -- or William. But at the time, I thought they didn't trust me. I didn't realize I was in even more shock than they were.

They sent me to a small room next to the nursery, with instructions to open the curtains so they could watch me. William and I got along fine. I had loved feeding his older brother; and I loved all babies. I knew in my heart, that loving him was not going to be a problem. Furthermore, I wasn't about to let those nurses see me have any problem with feeding my son. How hard could it be anyway!

You can't imagine. At least I never could have imagined. Without suction, the formula just ran everywhere. I had no idea how much was entering his mouth, let alone actually being swallowed. It looked to be scant, to say the least. Without ears, William looked like a small bird. He was tiny, precious, and like all babies, so vulnerable. Unlike most babies, however, he had formula, not dripping, but running from his chin.

Grief-in-limbo acts as complicated grief because it lacks discreet exit points. William is different, not dead. All grief-in-limbo can keep doing is chase "different" around in a circle.

I was happy for William's life; I had come to cherish life. I was happy to want to breathe again. His life was not the trauma of Dad's death. I figured (correctly, so far) that if I lived through the murder of my father, I could live through about anything. On the other hand, this was nothing like I had ever experienced, or have since.

Grief-in-limbo is the constant pendulum between loss and life, nearly equally balanced because "moving on" becomes continually and severely interrupted. With every forward movement, there is a constant reminder of the loss that is pulling you back, close to the place of beginning again.

The full story of William is a profound teaching, and a separate story that doesn't belong here. During his first twenty-two years, he lived with me, but now he lives semi-independently. He has overcome much; and there is much he will never overcome. Definitively, we still have to come back to William's handicapping conditions, upon which all decisions are at least partially based.

Identifying the early losses included: Loss of normal (again). Loss of sense of security (no knowledge of this kind of parenting). He wasn't growing on the formula (no knowledge of his need for a more specific diet). No nursing him (no one suggested pumping my breast milk for him). No support from professionals (one Army Nurse came to the house one time, said she thought we were doing fine, and never came back). Some of the best pediatricians in the world couldn't understand why he wasn't gaining weight. He weighed only 11 pounds at ten months. (Loss of knowledge) Then, my husband was assigned to duty in Viet Nam when William was six months old. (Unavailable parent partner.)

Thank God for Edith. She was nosy, blunt, and pushy. She took one look at William, asked what was wrong, and prescribed her Shaklee product for him. She wasn't a doctor, but she turned out to be right. On the Shaklee Instant Protein, William gained five pounds in a month (more than he had gained in the previous ten). Sometimes it is hard to accept the way God brings what we need into our lives.

Desparately, I began studying nutrition as if I was the starving person instead of William. In a way, I was the starving person, for knowledge, balance, resolution, hope, and understanding. Soon I knew more about nutrition than his doctors, which caused an entirely new level of loss. I lost "someone ahead of me."

It sounds strange, but I studied nutrition for 16 hours of lectures under an Egyptian who had a master's degree in Vitamin E. I told you it sounded funny. Later, this man tried to convince doctors in America that nutrition would make the difference in dying patients, based upon his research with the enzymes produced by the organs as a by-product of their functioning. He was allowed to work with "terminally ill" patients. I guess they figured, "How could he hurt them?" Then these terminally ill patients would get well, and the doctors would say they were "misdiagnosed." They said the patients weren't really terminally ill afterall.

The man who taught me nutrition went on to medical school, and was allowed to teach his nutritional ideas to medical students for up to seven hours of lectures, while he was getting a Degree in Medicine himself. Meanwhile, he reported to us that the American Medical Association buried his research under so much legal impasse that it would be years before we would hear of it. That was thirty-four years ago! I only began hearing about enzymes related to the heart organ (Mom's), a few years back, and then for the purposes of assigning more medication, not for treating with nutritional supplements.

However, this unusual slip in the western medical gears, brought a glimmer of light, that was enough to help William to grow. In fact, several times in his life, we were to discover that he would thrive on healthy food, and never do well on food high in refined sugar, or highly processed foods. Another problem emerged, however. Possibly because his brain did not get enough protein his first year, or for whatever reason (continued loss of knowing answers), we discovered that William is mentally retarded.

Questions flooded my already saturated mind. Will he learn to read? What will he be able to learn? Will he ever take care of himself? Will he graduate from high school? The good news is: William forgets he is mentally retarded, which may mean that he is okay with his life as he lives it.

The bad news is: William forgets he is mentally retarded, and continually sets himself up for disappointments. It is the same pendulum, always going back and forth between what we can find to be grateful for, and what is renewed loss, and therefore contributory to grief.

There is life outside of William, but for everything to do with William, life is fringed with grief, the same way a beautiful puffy cloud can intermittently block out or reflect the sunshine. That is the definition of grief-in-limbo. There will always be one more thing to learn that William cannot or will chose not to be able to do. While he climbs uphill, and continues to learn new skills, he slides back down the hill, losing ground somewhere else.

William lives in his own living space, with the help of an organization designed to help the handicapped, but of course he forgets he is handicapped at times, and they stress his independence. So we swing back and forth between trying to help and protect him, and just leave him to his own choices. Right now, he volunteers at an animal shelter, and he works part-time for a church, but mostly he lives off Social Security. In 2042, William will be 72, if he lives that long, and he's strong as a horse, so there is no reason to believe that he won't. Social Security might not live that long. He is in good health now, but the people monitoring him often allow him to choose his own groceries, so I don't know what he is eating. And by now, he may have forgotten again about the nutrition he needs. In fact, I can count on that.

When I was a child, there was an elderly woman in our church who had an adult, mentally handicapped son, named Bob. They came to church together. They seemed to do everything together. She died first, of course. I don't know who took care of Bob after that. Death, under such circumstances, may not be your worst nightmare. Death, at times, can be freedom from all kinds of pain and grief.

It seems to me that my pain of grief-in-limbo has to be continually monitored, so that fear does not dominate this kind of grief. This means, once again, letting go of fear. Giving to God the charge of my son happened one day in my front yard.

William was in the 7th grade, and he had to cross a very busy street to get to his junior high school. He liked riding his bicycle to school, despite not being real steady while riding it. There was real and possible danger as well, for drivers who wouldn't know that he was hearing impaired.

I would go to the front yard each morning to see him off to school. After he left, I would stand there for awhile to listen for squealing tires or sirens, in case he was in an accident. One day I decided I was being ridiculous. My thinking followed this exact route.

"God, I know that you love William more than I will ever be able to, and I am just going to have to trust you to get him to school." I never waited for the sound of sirens again.

Acknowledgment of God's love being forever greater than mine, and my true helplessness to control things I cannot change, has helped many times to neutralize my grief-in-limbo. By definition, it won't go away, but it can become minimally stressful. Once again, *my big gray buddy* is ever present, a familiar companion in life with me, **but not in charge**.

When grief about, or for, William becomes bigger than the importance of his person, I find support. I use my voice to reconnect to my spirit and the Great Spirit of God.

I may come through any doorway possible -- I may ask, cajole, vent, cave, cry, bare my soul, sing, or simply share my truth with one other human. Anything, to be restored to my being and my belonging to God. Being is the one thing I must have in order to continue to mother William in a healthy way. And when I can no longer mother William, God will find others who will, just as this provision has been in place ever since he was born. I do gratefully remember Edith.

Encouragement for Caregivers (page 187) picks up where this chapter ends. Grief-in-limbo is a huge component of the continuing losses felt by those care givers and care receivers inside the sometimes long and arduous transitions through aging and terminal illnesses, as well as handicapping conditions.

Being realistic about my abilities,
myself as a resource to others,
my limitations, and my humanity --
helps to keep me humbly alive.

It is the best gift I can offer,
and I learned it in limbo....

right after I learned to keep breathing.

Child for This Season

Child for this season, my mysterious son,
Dances in prisms of the crystallized young.
Laughing and loving, trusting everyone --
Such a long season, under each day's sun.

Child in the rainbow, all colors of love,
Flies through his toyland - a soft-eyed dove.
He stretches my loving -- dusk until dawn,
After a storm, wide-eyed, he'll yawn.

Child in the snowflake, falling and turning,
Humming a tune he hopes I am learning,
Slow motion unfolding, he melts in my arms
One in a million, who robbed him of ears,
but then, gave him his charms?

Child for this season, but what about next?
What tempest, what turmoil next season
begets? -- nevermind right now,
Enjoy today's fun, with this wonder-child,
Forever young.

k Ah

TEN

Mind and Body

At a very young age, Betty Buckman began assisting her teacher in the small country school she attended. There wasn't enough school work for her grade level to keep her bright mind busy. For several reasons, this experience appears to be of noteworthy influence. For one thing, it taught Mother to share and care for others in her earliest years. It was also the beginnning of being organized. She did her own work, and then helped others to do theirs. Ultimately, she moved through the grades effortlessly, her teachers paying little attention to the detail of her age. As a result, she entered the larger town school ahead of her peers, and graduated from high school at age 15.

Mother told us that from the age of 8, she wanted to be a librarian. She graduated from Denver University at 19, and accomplished earning her Master's Degree in Library Science the next year. Most people knew she was smart, but she seldom flaunted just how smart (except when we would do crossword puzzles together, or she would read a book in an evening.) Even then, she was just being herself; I was just jealous. It is ironic, to me, that she would have been one of my most efficient proof readers for this book, had she been alive. Of course, if she were alive, I wouldn't be writing this book.

The few times I remember Mom really struggling in her job as Weld County Library Director, was either when she had to fire someone, or the time when her Board of Directors hired a so-called efficiency management team. My generally, soft-spoken, unruffled mother was livid at the decisions made by the efficiency team. Her staff, who behaved as an intimate family, cheerfully attending their tasks, were harrassed and timed and all but accused of loitering and wasting time all day...under my mother's supposed inefficient watch!

Mother's blood pressure rose, literally. She was the biddy throwing a fit over a snake in the hen house. The board backed off the time management idea, although I was too preoccupied in my teenage years to really know what she did to have this happen. I think it was more than the coffee cake she baked for every board meeting.

Mom's intelligence also created a burden; she did not forget much. I think it played a part in the stress on her heart over the years. Consider how many persons now live into their eighties, as did my mother, who have had two to three heart surgical procedures. Modern medicine is indeed miraculous.

At the same time, living longer calls us into a stronger awareness of the need to be comfortable with aging, and all of its challenges. Mom tried harder than anyone I know to grow old gracefully, but I knew certain things disappointed her. Of course, she was always saddened when her friends died. She was sorely disappointed in most Republicans, and she was unhappy with her legs not being able to trot through her last years the way they had through her first half century.

As people age, their minds naturally slow down, and so did Mom's, I think. It was sometimes hard to tell because Mom's "slower" brain seemed faster than the fastest brains of others. I noticed her speech becoming less punctual and clear, as if her words slightly ran together. Causally, it might have been her medicines for her heart, her aging, or small strokes we never knew about. She didn't use alcohol, except a glass of wine with dinner now and then, and no alcohol while Dad was alive.

I never understood why Dad was so opposed to any alcohol use, until I learned that his dad drank too much when Dad was a child. He would just tell me how terrible alcohol tasted. It is anyone's guess how old he was when he first tasted alcohol. When he and mom visited us in Germany, he tried one beer and one glass of wine. He wasn't fond of either, but every town in Germany has their own brewery, so there's a prevailing, incidious temptation that we each had to try a few times.

Both Mom and Dad thoroughly enjoyed visiting Germany, and seeing the world they had heard so much about during WWII. Dad had nearly died during the War years, from kidney disease. It disqualified him from fighting overseas, but not from long hours of teaching young soldiers on their way to serving in the military. In fact, perhaps his entire life as my father was about living on "borrowed time." The discovery of sulfa drugs saved his life. I am grateful for the twenty years I had.

After Dad was killed, Mom traveled a lot more. Her mind expanded into an amazing awareness of places she had seen, foods she had eaten, and books she had read along the way. For years she was an excellent "boss." Then for even more years, she was an excellent "volunteer." Either way, Mom fit well into a world dominated by mental prowess. The sedentary, mental lifestyle has its price, which was part of her pain and weakness her last few years. Her physical struggle was probably due to never being very physically active, and the genetic predisposition to heart disease.

Medicine doesn't specialize in the treatment of awareness so much as prolonged existence, with mixed results at times as to the quality of life. Western medicine mostly worked well for Mom's agenda. She wanted to stay alive. However, not without quality.

She would go into surgeries and medical remedies with a positive burst of energy, and a knowledge she would be okay when all was said and done. She wasn't worried. If she died, she had her life in order, her DNR (Do Not Resuscitate) instructions, and her faith in place. Her willingness to "go the distance" medically, may have contributed to her doctor's confused response when she began to let go of her life so easily. She had always appeared to be a fighter. He didn't know this calmly capable person who spiritually could let go, even though her mind insisted that she didn't know how to do this.

At a certain point, medicine can create a paradoxical indication. A side effect, for example, of anti-depressant medication can be depression. Likewise, sometimes heart medication begins contributing to the heart's problems. Doctors find themselves in the middle of this dilemma. Several months before mother died, this contraindication of medicines began happening for her. By then, she was taking thirteen medications, of which no one was completely certain of their virtues. I am still grateful to the one cardiologist who was honest with me about this.

The function of the mind, as we know, does much to control bodily functions. In the experience of a slow death, however, one sees the separation of these functions. The healthy moving forward into life is the integration of body, mind and soul, and the exit appears to be the mirror image; the separation of the body, mind and soul.

The mind goes to confusion, fog, disinterest, sleepiness, fatigue, and not knowing. Who can tell what begins to captain the ship under these circumstances. In the end, mother's spirit was willing, her mind was perplexed and worried that she wasn't letting go the right way, and her body went mindlessly into survival mode.

The final stage of the body's attempts to survive are represented by the feet and hands becoming cold, and the blood being conserved for the vital organs, especially the heart and the lungs. As the blood is conserved for the vital organs in the chest, some blood is left behind in the extremities. This remaining pooled blood in the arms and legs appears as brown spots.

Despite Mom having had Congestive Heart Disease for years, in the final hours it was her heart hanging on to the last of her strength and blood. Her chest was burning hot with this effort, and she threw off the sheets we delicately placed over her naked body, from which she had already stripped any gown we gave her to wear. Finally, we allowed her the dignity and beauty to be as naked as she chose. There she was -- peacefully sleeping, her beautiful, soft and sagging breasts, rosy from the effort of her heart to continue pumping, rising and falling with her shallow, labored breathing.

We watched, smiling, tenderly crying, and murmuring

small devotions. I was fascinated by the rhythmic stretching and reaching of her arms through the air, like a ballerina dancing into her next life, or a swimmer making her way across the Jordan River. Whether she was conducting a symphony in her sleep, or swimming through her next birth canal, or simply doing what her confused mind was instructing, she would come to a halt at times, cupping her hands full of air, and bringing them to rest on her bare torso. I could not miss the parallel death seemed to birth when I witnessed it in this slow motion. While I knew she was dying, I couldn't help thinking she also appeared to be going somewhere, and I wondered exactly where.

Rapid, violent deaths probably have components of this transition, but we don't often see it, as fast as things happen. These deaths are more often exited through thrashing, crushing, gurgling sounds, ripping through a victim's surprised face. The body shuts down. We imagine the end coming so quickly that the experience is raw pain, but in shock, the body does not waste energy reporting pain. Quick, violent deaths probably step aside, disassociating from feelings as well.

As witnesses, we vicariously experience the violence, and all its opposition to being sensible. Perhaps our empathy and understanding must take up where theirs left. Perhaps we are to find the place of letting go that they would have found under better circumstances. Had my father lived to be 85, along with my mother, I can imagine that his dying process would have been very much like hers, where deep and peaceful sleeping would have been interspersed with laughter and crying with friends and family. Goodbyes would have been complemented by release of regrets, mingled with quiet times of bathing his perspiring body. Like hers, his small sighs, catching the middle of a breath, would have echoed our own fatigue and vigilance. Imagining this helps to mend some old wound inside of me.

Sudden, brutal deaths, such as those from car wrecks, plane crashes, murders, or suicides are unnatural deaths to us, and we are not prepared. In most cases, neither were they. The unjustness and unfairness of these deaths is harsh to us in every sense. The body will make every effort to survive. It does it automatically, but not necessarily from the place of pain. There are often questions about a loved one's suffering, but the body seems less involved with pain than survival if there is a question of the latter.

Mother had lived through so much, but awareness of her body was not a personal interest as long as her body was doing what she mentally wanted it to do. Before breakfast on Tuesday, she said, "It feels like everything is shutting down inside." It is important that this insight was nearly a first of its kind to come from her. I had never before witnessed such resonance between her mind and her body. She ate breakfast, and then threw it up. She never ate another full meal.

At the request of others, she tried to eat a little over the next few days, but she didn't want it. Eventually, even Mom's strong desire to please others took second place to what she truly needed. Her mind and body were two of three sleds coasting separately down a snowy hill. She was in and out of sleep. When she was awake, her mind was still on duty. Her body was in its own fight. There was blood in her urine. Her right arm hadn't worked for a couple of weeks.

This is what people do when they are dying. They stop eating, and they sleep a lot. While they appear to just be resting, we could also say they are working hard into their final transition. Naturally, they become dehydrated. I was told that the nature of the dehydration made Mom sleepier and less aware of pain. Mother did appreciate the little sponge suckers, however, that we dipped in water, and rubbed inside her mouth to keep it a bit moist. Meanwhile, the language was changing inside, from rejection of living to welcoming of dying.

It appeared that mother knew in her mind and in her body that the next right thing was dying. What I learned, watching her, was that the mind and body separate to accomplish this.

I witnessed this separation, and I had heard her childlike fairwell personally. I found this separateness comforting after her death, when I needed to think about her hair and make-up. My daughter, who had sold Mother her cosmetics for years, wanted to apply her Baba's final look. Likewise her hairdresser was honored to do Betty's hair one last time. I watched them lovingly prepare my mother's face and hair, I believe, just as Mom would have wanted it.

Mom's body served her well, as did her mind. In the final phase of living, however, it was Mom's spirit that took charge.

ELEVEN

Spirit

Despite my strongest attempts to believe the opposite, I believe I do have a Spirit. When Dad was killed, part of me died too. At the time, I thought it might be my Spirit that had died. I was too wounded to keep all of me alive.

I was young (21). I was hurt, vulnerable, lost, and overwhelmed by confusion. For a long time, I believed the part that was gone was my belief in God.

At the time of Dad's death, I was married to a man who called himself an atheist. I emulated him for his high intelligence. He seemed so much smarter than I was, or so I thought. Smart and Intelligence Quotient (IQ) are not the same, however. If wise people have the ability to learn from the mistakes others make, and smart people have the ability to at least learn from their own mistakes, then less than smart people must be the ones who do not learn from anyone's mistakes. Strangely enough, some less than smart people have high IQs. This may not sound profound to you, but I was a long time learning it, especially from the lost and wounded place I occupied.

I have made a lot of mistakes, many more than my mother did, but she was not 21, with her 3 month old son in her care, when her father was murdered. Where was I to find the parent to sustain me through such dark times, especially when my remaining parent was gasping for the same pockets of oxygen as I was. Mother and I resonated as motherless mothers in the same moment of loss. As Helen Reddy sang, "Who mamas Mama, who kisses away the pain?" We tried our best to be there for each other, but for a long time we were shadows of who we had been before Dad's death.

Like the cartoon characters, flattened by one of those asphalt highway rolling machines, I was one dimensional, deflated, nearly flat-lined - barely breathing. I knew I would never be the same after Dad was killed. How do we get from devastated to renewed? Nothing is going to be the same again. We cannot go back; life doesn't work in reverse the way a DVD player can. We can't put life on *pause* until we catch our breath...or can we?

Doesn't something like slow-motion pull us through the days when we have lost all sense of direction and connection to others? Time passes, things change, while the mute button has stilled our singing voices. The music is silent, but others are still dancing. They nod as they pass by, and somewhere deep inside, there is a memory of laughter and life before trauma. It is the innocence for which every wounded person longs, yearning for that time before the dreadful pain. I believe this yearning comes from our divine Spirit, and Spirit will let itself be known. Whether on the wings of nature, a kitten's small cry, or our own, Spirit returns us to life.

One way is through the voice speaking truth, into the ear that hears, and the eye that sees, and we turn to the whisper of life, and we heal. It is a miracle how it happens, but be assured it does happen -- to people who are miserable, those who believe and those who do not. The difference is this, between those who believe and those who do not. Those who believe find peace. Those who do not believe will continue to ask questions to which they already have the answers.

"What is this calm I feel? Should I kill it off? Is it another emotion to destroy?" After the caring friend gently laughs and says, "That's serenity, don't kill that one," the wounded non-believer will still wonder about what might be missing. "Are you certain?" they ask.

Whether one believes or not, it is in the turning, watching, and listening that we heal. God doesn't have to be believed in to work miracles in your life, but one has to be listening and watching to *get* that a miracle has happened. Peace follows "getting it." Oddly enough it is about this simple, but much easier to say than to do. Healing is not easily accepted from our human perspectives.

Unfortunately, even my experienced voice can sound empty to a currently traumatized person. Even to a traumatized person who wants to believe and to regain their lost hope, our voices will sound, at best, like a bell on a distant shore. It is through their own soul's voice that they will begin to hear the echoes of the beauty they were created to have -- before their loss of innocence, before the ugliness of violation faked contaminating their beauty, and before their knowledge of being loved crossed wires with feeling abandoned.

Only the holiness in healing can undo the fusion. Only the divine within us knows to try, despite failing over and again from our best human efforts. This abandonment to healing is the soul's finest hour. The soul that knows God's love also knows to love again. We go forward via life and breath, memory and voice, healed and re-created by our souls, appearing to free-fall without a parachute. This posture, otherwise known as faith, cannot be contrived. It comes on wings of doves flying through portals in the eyes. It comes on the sound of water flowing over the lashes and down the cheeks. It comes in knowing it is safe to risk feeling feelings again. It comes in recognition of the deeply familiar essence inside.

Unreceptive

One of the big problems happens when wounded people shut down their receivers, but they have to, at first. Facing all the pain at once seems lethal (and maybe it is, because many of the wounded die.)

In more than 11,000 hours of counseling, I have not met a wounded person who didn't shut down, at least for a season. A kind of shock, shutting down is an adjustment to the seemingly never-ending ripples of losses. Every reminder of loss is another ripple. In my case, every wonderful thing my beautiful son learned during his first year of life both thrilled me, and filled me with the reminder it was something my dad would never see.

Dad had been so happy being able to hold my son when we brought him home from Germany at two months old. One month later, Dad was dead. My son probably saved my life that year, because he was a constant reminder, pure and innocent, of the essence of goodness, but he and I both paid a terrible price for my mental absence.

My husband knew something was wrong between

my son and myself. He would mistakenly say things like, "You never did get along with each other." It was years before I understood what had really happened. Due to my disconnection from life, my son and I didn't fully bond emotionally, as mothers and sons need to do. Sometimes there is still an absence, where connection should be. It is a terrible price to pay for something that neither of us could have prevented.

My son was my hope, dancing out on the water ahead of me, the shiny, glistening sparkle that lured me into believing in living for another day. It is supposed to be the other way around, where a happy, smiling parent beckons the child into the richness and safety of living. Wounded parents automatically set their children up for missing part of their childhood, as the children take on a responsibility for which they are not equipped.

Slowly, I awoke to life, but for many months, when I held him, I wasn't fully there. I looked "there," but part of me had died. My son grew up in the arms of a partially alive person. Thankfully, my husband's mother often held our son. Maybe she was not as caring as I would eventually become, but at the time she was more alive. It must have felt like I was waving to him from afar -- a one dimensional mother, like a flag in the wind, a painting on the wall. What a terrible loss for us both, until we could begin to turn, to see and hear, and heal. Because of the Spirit inside each of us, this process of healing continues, and is alive as long as we are.

Mother's process of dying brought my son and me back together after an especially difficult time in our lives. She wanted peace between us, and for her sake, we made it happen. She let me know how proud she was of herself for simply being the one we came together for, and I don't begrudge her such a holy posture.

This is that powerful being/doing connection in the middle of loving life. Despite the enormous involvment in the process of dying, she could still *do* living right up until the parting "Goodbye."

Dying is the essence of being that slips through a sacred straw, the mystery of which we can only watch like a fog disappearing into sunshine. Some part of Mom seemed to know exactly what was going to happen for all of us, the peace of which she showed us by thoughtfully, and calmly disappearing through the veil.

Her death did not bring the pain of deep wounding. This was no parallel to the experience of Dad's death -- no stabbing wound. It was, in fact, the opposite.

I was present. Happily, I was there to receive.

I opened up from my inside; from my heart to hers. I felt like a big peace rose in a sunny garden, wishing my mother well on her journey. I knew I would miss her. I still do at times. Even two years later, I head for the phone to call her, and remember I cannot. Then I hear her wisdom, and in my mind I see her example, and my memory of her is free of pain.

Of course I have discovered ripples off such a primary loss, but if I keep my receiver open, I have options and choices to consider. Sometimes I am challenged by the choice either to shut down again, or to open my receiver to the intimidating miracles of life.

Years ago, during my early skills of opening up my wounded receiver, to what is sacred and holy about life, I experienced an extreme emotional draining, and physical exhaustion. My body and mind could barely keep pace with my spirit's desire to mend. Now, today's lesser topics for healing are less tiring. My healing has always seemed to be about calming the inner battles between what I know in my mind, what I feel in my heart, and what is intuitive to my spirit. As I mature in these areas, perhaps more integrated now than ever, the battle is more often just a disagreement, but I remember when the inner distances felt like chasms inside of me.

The Mind is predictable, the Body is tangible, but what is the Spirit?

Is the Spirit elusive and fleeting, or do we get in the way of seeing our souls with our creative doubts? Is it illusory, deceptive, imaginary, or do we simply have trouble finding it? What if Spirit is a personal and living experience with a larger force than our own? Scriptures tell us that God is invisible and inaudible unless you have *eyes to see and ears to hear.* Those sound like acts of living. I don't think that is in reference to hallucinations so much as illumination. I have a sense of my spirit; mother had a sense of hers. I believe our final parting represented our combined experiences of mind and body, guided by the interpretation of our Spirits.

The visceral experience of my mother's death was blood in her lessening urine output, that showed failure of her kidney function. Her body's perspiration smelled of the toxic waste building in her bloodstream. The physically hard work of trying to survive against the odds was evidenced, and all my senses screamed, "Mother is dying."

My mind held onto the illusion of control as long as possible, or as long as it was healthy to do so. Denial is a powerful, but not always healthy function of the brain. It acts as a steel door against the Truth of Death. If the truth of death is symbolically represented by the wind and the rain, where the wind represents the Spirit, and the rain represents emotion, then death can come as a mist or a torrential hurricane. It is my sense I have experienced both.

My Spirit took the information from my mind and body sensors, experiencing my mind's desire for control, and my body's responses to the visceral. In the emotional mist, my Spirit pointed to the presence of God. It was all so gentle, like my childhood experiences of a loving, ever-present God. I spent my childhood participating in youth activities with a Disciples of Christ church. I was especially active in my high school years. It was a community focused on gentle acceptance, potluck dinners, communion made of grape juice and small wafers, pastors who came and went, and parishioners who stayed a lifetime.

Dad's death didn't fit this country experience. When Dad was killed by a man who reported God told him to do so, my spirituality suffered a blow parallel to the brutality of Dad's murder. Much later I learned that the paranoid, and mentally and spiritually ill man who killed Dad had watched vampire movies repeatedly for more than a week. Wires seem to have crossed in his brain between the way a vampire has to die (on the night of a full moon with a wooden stake driven through his heart) and the way one stops the devil. He first stabbed Dad with a broken broom handle, and then returned to drive a wooden stake through his heart.

It took years to disconnect the association of my dad's

death with a full moon. I learned late in the afternoon of his death, over a plate of stuffed green peppers. We drove through the night across Kansas, a flat plain, looking all night like a silver platter in the moonlight. Ironically, when I drove by myself to spend (with her) what turned out to be Mom's final week on earth, I drove across Kansas under a full moon. As I traveled the country side, the gamut of emotions were like points on the compass. I touched base with every direction before settling calmly into the knowledge I was probably going home to say goodbye to my mother, and what a blessing that really was. I know what it is like to not have the priviledge of saying goodbye.

Even before Dad's death, I had no interest in vampire or horror movies, but certainly not since his death. Most importantly, I had serious repairs to make to my relationship to God. I limped along for a decade, before "retiring" to live in the mountains, at the ripe old age of 31. We moved to a small community of which I was one of the youngest adults in residence.

One day, three women in their seventies asked me to join their Bible Study. I smugly told them, "Okay, as long as we don't have to talk about God."

They said, "Okay, what would you like to talk about?"

Stunned, I had to think a moment. My attention turned to the wind blowing, as usual, and I blurted out, "the wind."

Looking back, that seems pretty funny. It was God's way of coming through my tightly built log cabin, literally -- and through my sealed-shut spiritual house as well. Do you have any idea how many verses in the Bible mention the wind? We never had to study anything else! There is much wind in the Bible and there was much wind in my life, every bit of which was needed to blow away the cobwebs of my trauma.

They never lectured me on forgiveness. They never reminded me about how much God loves me, nor how much I needed to heal and give my anger to God, nor any of those other things I was not yet ready to hear. I barely had availability to the wind that howled through the pines, drifted the snow, and cleared the air of the firewood smoke. I can still feel the cold wind on my face, forcing my eyes to water with emotionless tears, that would begin to prime the pump for returning to being human.

God is elemental. God is water, air, and light. One day, as the emotional glue in me began to soften, I found myself gasping for my own, personal, spiritual existence. God was my oxygen. I still cannot read "Footprints" without crying, because I understand it was during this time in my life that God carried me, and there was only His set of footprints crossing my desert, carrying me from a death worse than death itself, that of being lost and broken.

I began taking hope from anything with which my heart would resonate. A poem, a scripture, spring near a mountain lake, an elk's bugle, a child's laughter, a song, the sound of the snow falling, a remembrance. My understanding that I needed to heal began to save my life. The upward spiral began to replace the downward spiral I had been in for years. My mind made efforts to correct my course. My body grew stronger, having to work so hard in the thin mountain air. In those two years in the mountains, something healed enough, that I came back out of retirement and rejoined life with a determination to respond to my spiritual needs as well as my physical and mental needs.

Of course, I would be years attempting to fully integrate my mind, body, and spirit. Those were years filled with disappointments, poor therapists, ignorant and compromised priests, and more personal moments of hell, as well as a whole lot of growth. In the process of learning about healing, I managed to get kicked out of two different churches. In both cases, my voice, telling the truth and then sharing the truth was my biggest offense.

In one case, I was revealing a truth a priest did not want revealed, (about how much of the church's money he was spending) and in the other situation, I had gathered together some wounded women. We shared our painful stories. We began to feel better, sharing this way. (Recognize the grief work?) Church officials apparently felt threatened by my small voice, crying out for wounded children of God. Of course I left when they made it known to me that I was not welcome.

It is a sad commentary on churches who would shut their doors to anyone in need of healing, especially if they call themselves Christian (and both did.) My understanding is that our Lord came for healing the wounded. Churches that shut themselves away from people in pain indicate their own limitations and layers of woundedness. The churches of believers will always benefit by being the sharing place of grace, rather than judgment.

Wounded persons who are pushed away from hearing and watching (whether or not they know they believe) will go further into their unreceptive places. We will not bring God's miracle to those who need healing from painful losses by pushing them further away from the community of grace. I was one of the lucky ones, despite being asked to leave two churches. I made it to enough grace and peace to receive the blessing of my mother's death 35 years after my father's death nearly destroyed me.

The peaceful acceptance of my life as a spiritual, mental and physical existence was and continues to be held together by that sticky substance known as emotion. Writing, laughing, crying, and learning represent my movements through truth, even when the truth is painful to consider. Who is God that he allows so much bad to happen? What is the truth of God's love? I will always have some unanswered questions; I call it "my list" --the one I'm taking with me to heaven. Learning to live with partial answers keeps me more humble, and aware of my daily need for something and someone bigger than what I can do for myself. The wind?

Wherever you are will be wherever you are on your journey, when the truth of death challenges you with losses. I invite you to honor yourself as the elderly women of the mountain honored me. Your best in the present moment is good enough.

Present moment living will guide you in the process of both acceptance of the circumstances and acceptance of yourself. Awareness of your truth is more powerful than denial, even if you have come to rely heavily on denial. There is a saying in the recovery community, "Truth will set you free, but first it will make you miserable." Slightly more accurate may be "truth will set you free, but first you will realize how miserable you have truly been."

Acceptance of others, wherever they are on their journey, is essential. Acceptance was one of the things my mother did best.

Mother honored a person's need for time to heal. She seldom held feelings of guilt or inadequacy or unreasonable responsibility. She tried not to worry, even when she did not agree with what I was doing. In this way, her love lightened my load rather than creating more burden. (Remember the principle of agreeing to disagree.) Despite either of our strong minds urging to control, she, especially, remained open to possibilities and changes. These traits helped us to accept each other as the family struggled against time for the final moments of her life.

None of us used this time for insisting that others be more like us, or in burdening ourselves with being more like others. We worked to be true to ourselves as much as possible.

Ultimately, I sensed a truth of life and death residing among us, together in the place of humbleness. Nothing seems so humbling as loss and death. Time and again, we attempted to leave our expectations at the door, in order to walk into the full opportunity to be an intimate family gathered in respect, and yes, joy.

Symbolism

At her funeral, the four families came to the front, lit candles, and spoke words they had selected to represent their memories of Betty, Baba, and Mom. *Acceptance of others* was mentioned the most often. What finer definition of love might there be, than acceptance? How can one feel more understood, honored, and cared for, than to feel accepted?

Lighting candles refreshes this memory. The scent of vanilla brings back the hope and love we experienced the night she died. Symbols can represent the changes that occur in the heart.

Mother did not confuse acceptance with agreement. She was free to disagree, but still accept the right for others to have a difference of opinion and belief than her own. This proved to be the glue within our family. Whether we were sick or healthy, controversial or traditional, classic or neo, silly or somber, sensible or absurd, Mother listened and learned before leaning hard into dialogue.

Then, she had a strong voice, but not a condemning one. What a gift! What glue for wounded individuals coming together to form a family.

This willingness of Spirit led her way toward a peaceful death, talking with others, and accepting herself, the way she had accepted others. Because it was a wonderful and strong habit by age 85, no one had to instruct her into her acceptance of her path. I watched. I admired. I learned. In the final days, she returned to the parent leading me. It felt like the completion of a perfect circle.

This is my story of Spirit, where religion is not central, but neither is it excluded. Religion is more about personal choice of rituals which at times seem to outline the presence of a God we thought was invisible. As importantly, I believe, is the coming to know of God's choice of us. The search for meaning is written in a thousand books more theological and better written than mine. I mention here some authors, some books, some discoveries, in an effort to provide more knowledge. I am biased about the need to read, and I believe that reading for spiritual growth is essential throughout our lifetimes.

The strength and presence of my mother's gentle life, drawn daily from her faith in God, and Jesus Christ, in her final days, as I've said, poured undiluted into the room. Each of us entered this holiness individually flawed by our experiences and fears, and chose whether or not to allow this concentrate of faith to test our inner wellness. Death does test ones metal. The loss of a loved one will test your truth, as it brings you face-to-face with your definition of meaningful living. For the wounded, this view may be into thousands of shards of mirrors made from tens of thousands of moments from which the pieces of your lives have been restored and glued.

An Invitation to Remember to...

Create symbols that remind you that miracles happen.
turn, see, and hear God's caring, and be healed.
accept yourself and others for where they are on the path.
See the foundation of life, built from spiritual, mental, and physical bricks, and Use healthy emotion as the mortar.
Know that despite trauma, your soul remains with you.
after becoming wounded, be patient with being shut down for a season,   Knowing your faith will return stronger, and more wise for your experiences related to losses.
Seek spiritual resonance by reading wise authors.
Invest in your well being with the abundance of truth shared.
(When you find an author you really enjoy, I encourage you to seek their other works, since only a partial list follows.)

Bibliography for Spiritual Reading

Melody Beattie, *Journey to the Heart; Daily Meditations on the Path to Freeing Your Soul.* (New York, NY.: HarperSanFrancisco, 1996)

Melody Beattie, *The Language of Letting Go; Daily Meditations for Codependents* (New York, NY.: Harper Collins, 1990)

David Benner, *Sacred Companions* (Downers Grove, IL.: InterVarsity Press, 2002)

Marcus Borg, *The God We Never Knew* (New York, NY.: HarperSanFrancisco, 1997)

Marcus Borg, *Meeting Jesus Again for the First Time* (New York, NY.: Harper Collins, 1995)

Forrest Carter, *The Education of Little Tree* (Albuquerque, NM.: Univ. of New Mexico Press, 1976)

Oswald Chambers, *My Utmost for His Highest* (Uhrichsville OH.: Barbour & Co., Inc., 1963)

Dorothy Day, *By Little and By Little: The Selected Writings of Dorothy Day* (New York, NY.: Alfred A. Knopf, 1983.)

Ed. Carol Dovi, *Gifts from Our Grandmothers* (New York, NY.: Crown Publishers, 2000)

J. Ruth Gendler, *The Book of Qualities* (New York, NY.: Harper & Row, Pub. Inc, 1988)

Thich Nhat Hanh, *Going Home; Jesus and Buddha as Brothers* (New York: Penguin Putnam, Inc., 1999)

Martin Luther King, Jr., *Strength to Love* (Philadelphia, PA.: Fortress Press, 1963)

Madeleine L'Engle, *The Rock That is Higher: Story as Truth* (Colorado Springs, CO.: WaterBrook Press, 2002)

Spirit

C.S. Lewis, *A Grief Observed* New York: The Seabury Press, 1961)

Max Lucado, *When God Whispers Your Name* (Dallas, TX.: Word Publishing, 1994)

Max Lucado, *Traveling Light: Releasing the Burdens You Were Never Intended to Bear* (Nashville, TN.: W Publishing Group, 2001)

Max Lucado, *In the Grip of Grace* (Dallas, TX.: Word Publishing, 1996)

Dawn Markova, *I Will Not Die an Unlived Life: Reclaiming Purpose and Passion* (York Beach, ME.: Re Wheel/Weiser, LLC, 2000)

Henri J.M. Nouwen, *The Wounded Healer; Ministry in Contemporary Society* (New York: Doubleday, Image Edition, 1990)

Henri Nouwen, *Turn my Mourning into Dancing: Moving Through Hard Times with Hope (Nashville, TN: W* Publishing Group, 2001)

Rita Reynolds, *Blessing the Bridge; What Animals Teach us about Death, Dying, and Beyond* (Troutdale, OR.: NewSage Press, 2001)

Albert Schweitzer, *Reverence for Life* (New York: Harper & Row, 1969)

Brian Luke Seaward, *Stand Like Mountain Flow Like Water Reflections on Stress and Human Spirituality* (Deerfield Beach, FLA.:Health Communications, Inc., 1997)

Marianne Williamson, *Illuminata* (New York: Random House, 1994)

-147-

...out of money, out of spit, out of focus, out of grit ...off my spelling, lost my mind, off my timing, out of rhyme, out of sync, past my prime ... I am. I'm...

outside the target
full of myself
unexcused
partially
indignant
right or not
where is enough
faith, belief,
hope
perserverance
acceptance,
patient
confidence,
guts, solitary
or together.
How and when
will this end?

am

enough

On fingertips, not tips of tongues, around a sharp-edged paradigm, a shining in the next right thing, lightening up the stormy sky -- it is I,
        all the I that I can be.

A Sampling on Patience

For all my life, my mother was a librarian. She had a cup that read "Librarians don't die, they just check out." I grew up loving to read. I want to share the book I read that helped me out of my deepest confusion. I read and re-read at my kitchen table, every day for three years, from *My Utmost for His Highest* by Oswald Chambers. He puts words together I never heard others say, such as "the passion of patience." His own passion for patiently explaining life became my morning (and my mourning) sustenance.

He wrote:

--patience is not indifference; patience conveys the idea of an immensely strong rock withstanding all onslaughts. The vision of God is patience, because it imparts a moral inspiration. (p. 123) Ultimately, for me, his thoughts helped to restore me to both patience and God, and my enoughness.

TWELVE

Wellness

There is a difference between living a good life and living into the wellness of your being. The risk of focusing only on a good life, is that of becoming a bean counter. Mother had the opportunity to become a bean counter. She had several plaques on her wall that represented just a few of many awards and achievements she received during more than 30 years as a professional, 20 years as a volunteer in retirement, and 75 years as a member of her church.

At church, Mom had performed nearly every job but the pastor's, only because she had lived so long, not because she was aggressive. She never wanted the pastor's job. In fact she was one of the first of two women who were asked to become elders, who both turned down the honor. She reported, "I liked watching the men up there, and I thought if the women were to become elders, the men would find a way to serve less often." (It is tempting to digress on that quote, but I think it is outside the scope of this book.)

Mother graduated from high school at the age of 15. Possibly if her peers had recognized her more personally at the time, her life would have turned out differently. As it was, she missed having more friendships in high school, and spent the rest of her life assuring others that they mattered to her. Subsequently, she accomplished a great deal in a quiet way; never in an attempt to outdo anybody else. She was seldom competitive. While she was happy to be honored with an award or recognition, she was humbled, and privately hoping no one resented her for it. I found certificates of merit at the bottom of stacks of dusty and unremembered papers. Her legacy was that many people came to me privately, to say simply, "She was a good friend to me."

When Mom announced to her doctor that all she had to do was to "let go now," he appeared to quietly accept her imminent death. He asked her if she wanted to have any pain medication. She assured him truthfully, I believe, that she wasn't in any pain at the time. Mom thanked her doctor for being a good doctor to her over the past several years they had known each other. He said, "Yes, we've been through a lot together." She thanked him again, to which she received a shrug. The third time she thanked him, I touched his elbow and suggested it would be okay to say, "You're welcome."

"It's hard to say," he said, awkwardly. Perhaps because he knew it meant "goodbye."

It seemed the professional in him wasn't used to digging into those personal feelings to share his hopes for a sweet and successful passing, especially not directly to a patient who was sharing her willingness of Spirit to die now. It was no longer about his medicine giving her hope. She was offering him something better -- an opportunity to grieve and to celebrate at the same time, simply as humans together.

What does one say? "Happy trails to you...until we meet again...hum?" I'm thinking.

"I'll miss you." No, it's dismissive.

"Have a good time." Really!

"I'm sorry I cannot help you more with this part." That's a start -- at least it's honest.

"I'm glad your family is here with you, as they have always been." Not really a personal comment to her, since it is not really about their relationship.

Here is what I want from my doctor, when I am at death's doorstep (especially if he is as good looking as Mom's doctor.) He'll take my hand, come close to me, and look me in the eyes, and say: "I have so enjoyed having you as my patient. I respect you, your dignity, and so much about you, including your sense of humor (and this fantasy you left for me to say to you.) If you need it, you have my permission to die. I have no more medicines that will change your status of life. I have done my best for you."

"Yes, you have," I will confirm.

"So, I say fondly and sadly, goodbye. And just in case you are still alive when I am around here in a couple of days, I'll drop in and say all this again to you -- as often as I need to, because this is all the treatment I have left for you in my little black bag. It is called closure." Then of course, since this is my fantasy, he would kiss me on the forehead before leaving, and saying his final "Goodbye."

In real life, many professionials are not prepared for the transition of moving from a professional climate into an intimate one, such as dying presents.

Her doctor said,"You're welcome, Betty, call me if you need anything." This was not closure; this was not "Goodbye, Betty. Thanks for letting me be part of your life experience." He left a prescription of tylenol in case she had any pain, and he made sure it was liquid, since she wasn't able to swallow much of anything. These were kind considerations, but not closure. We could see that he was visibly touched by her departure, yet emotionally unequipped to join Mom for the tender moment.

Her minister also struggled. He came to her bedside, sat quietly in the corner, watched the family interact with visitors, and witnessed people experiencing their personal closures with mother. One woman from the church made a surface effort by ignoring the suggestion to say "goodbye" with jokes about what she did that day. We accepted this as her limitation. It was as if this woman stepped up to the great lake of intimacy in the room, and quickly backed away, the topic of dying too big, too wet, or too deep for her that day. She poked fun at herself for awhile and then left.

Shortly after that, Mom's minister jumped up and offered to pray. While they were nearly the only words he spoke during his visit, they were eloquent and graciously filled with gratitude for mom's life among us. Then he burst from the room. I followed him to the elevator to be certain he was all right. I put a hand on his shoulder, and said, 'it's okay to grieve with us." He was crying. And then he was gone. I have no idea if he was sad for himself, his life, his own losses, or the loss he felt in Mother's passing. He did not invite any of us into his private space of grieving. Grief unshared remains a mystery.

If you are uncomfortable with what to say about dying, you are not alone. Even professionals that deal with death frequently can experience the loss awkwardly. Our society doesn't spend much time planning for these moments, but we need to. We truly need to prepare ourselves and our loved ones for these times. Wellness is about:

- being able to live with change,
- living within intimate and vulnerable realities,
- accepting ourselves in our vulnerability,
- sharing our vulnerable selves when appropriate,
- knowing the appropriate from the inappropriate,
- knowing ourselves well enough,
- handling the race straight through the finish line,
- and finding gratitude and relief in the process.

The wellness of the Betty Buckman Adcock Bowers family was extended to Mom by her grandchildren, some of whom were able to be present to say goodbye to their "Baba." The ones who were too far away to visit personally were kept informed. Every member of the family was given options. Some wanted to remember another time and circumstance than the one of her dying. Others came to have a final conversation. The indicator of their wellness was partly in their ability to share their desires.

When the youngest grandchildren, two boys ages 10 and 13, entered her room, she was sleeping. They sat next to her bed in bewilderment, until I suggested it would be okay to hold and stroke her hands. I explained that apparently she was still being comforted by this. They were grateful, and with hands like "kitty paws" each softly stroked a hand.

Mother had taught us to accept whatever level of wellness and courage a person could express. She never spoke this instruction. She had simply demonstrated it in a thousand ways over the years. Her way hung in the room with her gently lingering essence. The generations abided, moment-by-moment, in the understanding that whatever degree of wellness any of us could muster, was enough.

The wellness of one's being might be demonstrated in the intelligent way one deals with problems, or the physical way that one deals with disease, or the spiritual way one deals with loss. Mother was blessed to experience a high degree of wellness in all of these areas, which may help to explain why she was clearly dealing with the demise of all three of these at once. As her energy waned, however, her spirit, mind, and body began to take their separate courses.

Her Spirit was willing, as evidenced by her announcement to her doctor, she would no longer be taking her medicines because she no longer needed them. "I just have to let go now," to which her organizing part of her mind responded with, "I don't know how to do this." Her body was on a third course, unable to match with either mind or spirit. Survival is an instinct.

Wellness is about being able to live with change, and to live with the intimate realities into the vulnerability life inevitably draws us all, of which death plays a major role. As mother informed nearly everyone, "I just need to learn to let go now," some were stunned by her bluntness. She refused to participate in her final conference with the staff; she sent me instead. "You go. I don't want to, and I don't want them to meet in here either." So I went and I said, "My mother is dying, and I haven't done this before, at least not with my own mother. Please help me anyway you can." They did.

Resistance to this life, at some point, is part of the wellness of moving on. The nurses were unaccustomed to this level of accuracy about dying. Some warned us that sometimes people "last a long time in this condition." (And sometimes they do.) The staff would come in and ask her to come to dinner, even days after she had stopped eating.

Finally, they agreed to put the dove on her door (a symbol she was dying), which considerably helped to lower the level of noise coming from the hallway. As it became more evident to everyone that Mother really was dying, she was shown complete privacy and respect.

Wellness is about knowing the next right thing to do.

The month earlier, in August of 2003, I had come to visit, and Mom was using a lot of those little nitro tablets for her heart's pain. In the middle of the night, she rang her little bell, and I helped her to find another nitro tablet to take. Then I lay down beside her, thinking if she dies, she won't be alone. After about five minutes, she said, "I guess we are being silly to not call 911."

"Do you want to go to the hospital, Mom?"

"Yes."

So, I called the ambulance, and we went to the hospital, into a very busy Saturday night emergency room. They put her in the back of a side room, while they shuffled around some bruised young people in formal clothes. There must have been fifty of them who got into a fight that night. It was humorous in a way -- dressed up for Saturday night in the Emergency Room -- but, then I was still half asleep myself. I wondered what we were doing there.

Mom and I just sat quietly together, until she began having difficulty breathing. Her lungs seemed to be filling with fluid. I fetched a nurse who immediately began shooting a lot of stuff into my mother's veins. Mom began to look the color of paste. Around 2 a.m. I called my brothers and sisters to come. When they arrived, Mother was behind an oxygen mask, looking terrified. I am sure that I was mirroring this look despite my best efforts not to.

Six of us were staring at Mom, knowing she was trying not to drown in her own fluids, all believing we were looking at her final moments on earth. The thought that I could not chase from my mind was that Mother always had a fear of water. What if she has had this fear because she is going to die by drowning! Miraculously, she made it through that night, far less shaken by the experience, it appeared, than I was. I was angry. (Remember that coping with helplessness?) I had to leave in a couple of days to fly back home, before I knew whether or not mother would fully recover this time.

Mom didn't die that night. If she had, this book would not have happened. This miracle for me of the balance between my father's and mother's deaths would not have occurred. The story would have been: one parent was stabbed to death, and I watched the other one drown. I cannot expect anyone to understand the magnitude of my relief, in retrospect, but at the time, I thought, "Why didn't she just let go!" I thought that until she told me that she *had* prayed to God, "If this is my time, take me." It wasn't the next right thing, obviously, for any of us.

We cannot create wellness for others; we can only contribute -- or get in the way. Someone else's death is about their story; their instincts; their choices; their patterns of living. Mother's management of her death was at such a level of wellness, that a whole new construct was born in me. When she died, something in me gave birth. I gained an even stronger respect for a philosophy that includes sharing, learning, growing, consideration, acceptance, and wisdom, right up to the end. The following are some of the lessons we learned together. I invite you to look for the grief tiger's paw prints within the arena of wellness.

Granting Permission

Giving someone permission to die connects to the mental, physical, and emotional release that frees our loved one to do the next right thing. Since Mom's heart attack during the incident in the ER a month earlier, her best friend had come to see her daily. Permission worked both ways for them. The best friend needed permission to let go, and to stop coming by, and mother needed permission to not have to live one more day for her best friend. They had deeply shared over losses of their spouses, which added to the bittersweet understanding of this moment.

Then mother bluntly announced the names of the three children "holding me back." Perhaps it was her way of asking for permission from the three of us who were constantly there. My sister-in-law, who had buried her own mother just two months earlier, my brother, and myself were the named culprits. Of course, I was surprised to hear my name on the list. One by one, we leaned closely toward her soft, white face and whispered, "Mom, you have my permision to die." I was last, and afterwards she looked at me and said, "And you have my permission to die." I smiled. She laughed outloud. "I'm mixed up," she said, "you don't need that."

I didn't think about it much at the time, but as I write this, I am thinking maybe in her Spirit, she knew someday I might.

When she first announced that I was holding her

back, I was shocked really. I was the one who had gone to her Care Conference and announced that my mother was dying. I was the one who had called my siblings back to her bedside (more than once). I thought I was the one most prepared, and perhaps the most honest about the state of her health. The truth is, however, I hadn't actually spoken my permission to her directly, "Mom, it's okay to die now. I give you permission," which really means I give myself permission also, to let you go now.

Regrets and Confessions

My husband leaned over and quietly asked me, "Has your mother been given the opportunity for a confession? I stared at him blankly, wondering what in the world my sweet 85 year old mother would have to confess!

I answered, "Not that I know of."

He pursued. "Would you have any objection to my offering her this opportunity?" I had no objection, and we switched chairs, so that he could be nearer her face.

"Betty, sometimes people are held back in the process of dying because they have regrets they haven't expressed. Do you think you have any?"

"Oh, yes," said my mother instantly.

You really could have knocked me over with a feather. I sat stunned at the end of the bed, thinking how much trouble I would be in right now if I were the one dying instead.

The litany, albeit short, of Mother's regrets poured forth from her nearly effortlessly. You would have thought she had spent some time and thought on this, and maybe she had. It was a holy willingness to clean the slate.

It was so simple, the way it happened, that it was clear that her confession had come as the next right thing. Her regrets were nearly all connected to one family member. My brother heard her confession, and received her regrets. I wondered if I should even be in the room, the air itself seemed so holy. "Maybe the air is too holy to breathe," I remember thinking.

It wasn't that mother had done anything very wrong, but the sanctification was so real, followed by the obvious relief in Mom. Her burden was lifted from her heart. When she was finished, she simply stated, "That's all."

Mother and I had already worked through so much through the years, that I was pretty sure she didn't have any regrets related to me. I tried to think if I had any related to her. I was glad when I couldn't find any, and I felt a new respect for the process of intimately clearing up past issues as you discover them. Yet, I was riveted to the place of holy observance of a ritual our spiritual leadership has called us into for years.

Confession. Mom's "regrets" were more a sweet voice crying in the wilderness, clearing the way, or like a call to worship. It was a holy sacrament in a hospital room turned sanctuary. Afterwards, she rested quietly, while I sat amazed and honored by the obvious value of shared leadership within the family, taking the step together toward *good enough*.

Timing

Y ou may feel you are not ready for your loved one to die. Or you may feel willing, but they aren't. Or, you may feel unable to discuss this with your loved one. You may feel timid, reluctant, shy, or too scared to step forward. If this is the case, look for some help. Community is essential for gathering full wisdom. What to say when can often be confirmed by others.

Begin with your friends, who also know and care for your loved one. Not all your friends will be as shy or reluctant as you are about this topic of dying. Look for the friend who may have been through this with a loved one, but not too recently.

Find a bereavement counselor, or a social worker or specialist in palliative care or hospice, to guide you and other family members. Don't white knuckle this alone. Find some help. Ask the following kinds of questions directly to the person you choose to ask for help.

1. I think maybe (name) is dying. Do you think you are in a strong enough emotional place to support me through the process of losing (name)?

2. Do you have suggestions about helping me deal with the timing of this loss?

3. Do you know of anyone especially equipped to help me at this time?

4. What would be your suggestions of things to say and talk about with (name) at this time?

If you have a therapist, you might consider processing these kinds of questions:

1. Are you more frightened of living with the absence of this person in your life, or the actual process of being there for someone who is dying?

2. What part of the dying process do you fear the most?

3. What are some of the things you will miss most after this person has died?

4. What do you think this person expects of you during this time of their dying?

For spiritual direction, you may have questions about how to rely on God's strength, the importance of the dying person's beliefs and convictions, or questions of your own beliefs that crystallize suddenly around loss and death.

If you have trauma around death, you may fear death beyond the topic of your loved one dying. Dealing with this is important to do to experience wellness for your own life, and will greatly facilitate dealing with the death of another.

What if the person dying is also someone who has violated you in the past? This can bring up painful memories. While it may provide an opportunity for healing, it is probably best to process this with a trauma and grief specialist.

Consider a relative, friend, spokesperson, or mediator who could help to support and understand your situation and the vulnerability you both may feel. It is usually not wise to jump-frog to forgiveness if you have not at least talked to someone about the violation. Out of sync forgiveness, like putting the cart before the horse, may re-victimize you rather than lead directly to healing. Remember how unresolved grief can velcro to new grief, giving an appearance of the old loss happening again, or the new loss being unmanageable.

Many believe an ultimate healing happens when you die. You may hear "He won't be in pain in heaven," but imagining a loved one happy doesn't relieve our own pain. While we truly hope "he is not suffering now," the work of grieving is no longer needed by the one who has died. It is needed by those left behind and alive. The comment that the dead person is not feeling pain may remind those grieving of the already linked death to their own pain, rather than providing a comforting thought. In the listener's mind, there is, "Yes, and I am left behind with all this pain! Thanks for noticing!"

Because of the timing, you may feel abandoned by the person dying. Are you afraid to mention it because they can't help it they are sick? Talk this over with your support group. If you don't have one, ask your local church, hospital, therapist, or friends to start one. Talking about your losses is very important. Are you unable to change the timing of this loss? I invite you to deal with it head on, with honesty, help from others, and tolerance for your own place in the fog.

Lest you think my experience is unique, consider what my friend wrote of her experience. "My mother's death on Mother's Day was her gift of timing to us for she must have known even in her comatose state how unbearable it was for my sister and I to watch her suffer for another single minute. While my father and my brother were part of the death process, my sister and I were our mother's caregivers as we alternated staying nights with her at the hospital bedside every night from December 26, 1975 until her death on May 7, 1976.

Prior to her hospitalization, as mother struggled with cancer, and became less able to care for herself, I became her caregiver and our mother/daughter roles were reversed. And so, in the process of caring for my mother as she fought cancer, I learned from her, as she was a perfect example of how to live a life of love and die in faith. She was so strong and gracious in death, and on one particularly difficult and painful day, she said to me, 'I'm not afraid.' You cannot imagine how that statement has given me peace over the years." (Pat Ziegler, Nashville, TN)

Consequences

Often there is confusion about the difference between consequences and punishment, especially for those who have only been taught to fear God's wrath. Luckily, I didn't grow up focusing on damnation; which has freed me instead to focus on seeking God's love. However, I have experienced powerful lessons in what I would call obedience.

There do seem to be some natural laws established by God's order in the universe that, when broken, result in negative consequences and, when followed, result in positive consequences. **Then there are also things that make no sense at all.** Thinking we can know the fullness of God's thoughts, or even that he (or she) thinks the way we think, is surely arrogance. Because of a sense of my own limitations, I admit to having less interest in the topics of God's wrath and his punishment than I do in *natural consequences*.

Natural consequences happen as a result of behaviors we do for both a short time and a long time. The consequences of driving into a tree happens quickly. Behaviors that are subtle, such as smoking one cigarette at a time, will still result in a consequences of poor lung health, depending upon how long you smoke, your genetic predisposition, and other stressors in your life. Smoking cocaine has much faster and always dire consequences. Some of those consequences have to do with your body's health, some to do with your mind, and some to do with your finances. The consequences of repeatedly abusing yourself with drugs (or food or alcohol or sex or spending) ultimately is complete loss of physical and mental health, friendships, finances -- and ultimately -- loss of life.

Positive consequences can also happen. The person *empowered* to make healthy choices will evolve from the small child who feels accepted and loved. The person who carries this love and acceptance into adulthood as self love and self acceptance is able to balance out the bombardment of losses and the ensuing wake of confusion, mistakes, and doubt. Balance becomes a positive consequence.

Many addicts abuse themselves because they lack *freedom* to make the right choices, not because they do not know right from wrong. A negative consequence of neglect and abuse is the feeling of being a bad person. The positive consequence of being loved and accepted is the feeling of being a good and caring person.

Remember what Jesus said when people eagerly brought their children simply to be touched by him? "Let the little children come to me, do not hinder them; for to such belongs the kingdom of heaven." (Mt 19:14 RSV)

You will find a repeat of this incident in three of the four gospels that mention the correctness of blessing children, the incorrectness of hindering children, and the connection between the innocence of being a child and entering into the kingdom of heaven.

Jesus was indignant with the behavior of the disciples, who rebuked the parents who were eager to have their children blessed. Jesus overroad the poor judgment of the disciples, saying: Truly, I say to you, whoever does not

receive the kingdom of God like a child shall not enter it."
Then Jesus "took them in his arms and blessed them, laying
his hands upon them." (Mk 10:13-16 RSV) (and also Luke
18:15-17 RSV)

I had not thought ahead of time of scooping Mother
into my arms and rocking her in her final moments on earth.
I simply responded to some silent invitation that came at the
time. What was more natural than picking up this fragile
lady I so deeply loved, and holding her as best I could? What
was more natural than to say, "Bye, Bye?"

My amazement was that she responded. Nothing
had been uttered for hours from my mother's lips. How
much more evidence of holiness was I to ever need, than the
childlike voice saying, "Bye, Bye" back to me -- not once,
but three times? No more evidence is needed for me.

Holy is holy, and so there will always be mystery. Do
we go from birth to death through birth again? Maybe we are
children at every stage. Maybe the *child* in us is simply the
vulnerability that is always present. How more vulnerable
can one be than at the doorways of birth and death? One
being to gain everything, and the other to lose everything,
but which is which?

I love the Bible, in all its grayness, rather than the
black and white some try to paint it. Moments of clarity
do happen. They are bright spots of colorful flowers I can
also enjoy. Equally accepted and appreciated is the big, gray
ambiguity of life. Accepting the mystery of grief and loss
can release inside the peace that feels *enough*.

Good enough is well enough. Well enough is all we
need day to day. Well enough is not improved upon by
judgment or criticism. Well enough is improved by receiving

insights enthusiastically. Well enough blends in with honor and respect for the life-death dance. Today is enough. You and I are enough. Never mistake enough for too little. Never mistake enough for weakness, and don't push past enough by mistaking empty longing for the need for more than enough. There is abundance in enough, some call plenty.

Insecure bean counters contrive standards from numbers, absolute rules, and their extreme feelings, and seldom find the place of enough. As Mom stayed focused on doing the next right thing, she passed with grace, dignity, and wellness enough, to accomplish not only what she needed for herself, but also to bless those of us in her community. For this, I am eternally grateful.

time

the sweetness of its moments, or the bitterness to tell
sweet silence in its meaning, or the empty
        deep, dark hell.

mysterious, joyful journey – split painfully by losses
everything to nothing, evolves the changing forces

the time it takes for healing, finding Phoenix
        from the ashes

requires reporting life's true effort,
        seen through the looking glasses

Clarity, her voice up from the past
        smashes "time will heal"

It isn't true -- instead, the messenger in tears
        brings healing that will last.

kAh '03

THIRTEEN

Gratitude

Gratitude is the hinge on the door between the intellect and the heart. Padlocks and dead bolts swing wide, still tightly fastened to the intellectual defenses, when gratitude swings open this door. Misinformation, rationalizations, and cognitive distortions fade in the bright light of the soul that comes from the exposed heart.

The tiny hinge of gratitude is overlooked as a source for powerful change. Sometimes "it was a miracle," is the vague explanation for these changes happening. Maybe gratitude is the miracle. Or perhaps gratitude is unseen because kind persons often wear it like an invisible glove, and generous circumstances can generate gratitude in the form of oxygen to those in need. I think Mom wore invisible gloves of gratitude. Perhaps people subconsciously felt her touch in her soft-spoken strength. My husband especially felt this from her. When we traveled together, or she came to visit, he was appreciative of her undeterred benevolence. In simple generosity, Mother's actions were never without a show of sincere gratitude, that made it easy for us to be grateful in return.

Gratitude seems graciously, if not always conveniently, available in the inner workings of life itself. Hand in hand, grace and gratitude show up in the morning mist, on the first rays of dawn, from the chirps and beeps of the cardinals and chicadees, and the softly moving of one's heart into prayers of hope. Gratitude glides wordlessly on a newborn's smile that can melt the heart of a tired parent at three in the morning. Wherever gratitude is noted, received, witnessed, or acknowledged, life is altered for the better. It is not a replacement for the truth, but stylishly its handmaiden.

For example, during the season of Mother's death, my garden moved into Fall, wrapping itself in weedy grasses that would seed an entirely new crop of weeds the next year. The temptation was great to grumble about this, and add weeding to a list of things I could not possibly finish before the holidays, or even before the winter months in the South would come and go. Such lists can serve to fuel feelings of inadequacy, and thoughts of being deprived of enough time.

Oddly, on this day of discovering the weeds, I also re-discovered gratitude when I somewhat absent-mindedly stared out of my upstairs window and witnessed someone's (in this case, my own) beautiful garden. Brightly colored, changing leaves outlined the tall Crepe Myrtles, the volunteer River Birch, and the small but persistent Crab Apple tree, sprouting Fallish red berries for the first time.

Large, yellow oak leaves, and reddish brown of the Dogwood floated above purple waves of weedy grasses. A solitary, yellow lily signaled over the soft waves to an amazingly bright, white reblooming iris, equally proud and alone. Sparkling dahlias crawled into the path, and tropical cannas stood like loyal, forgotten soldiers, with little red plumes for hats. The many birds wove flight patterns over a grounded chipmunk, representing the visiting wildlife, none of whom complained to me the way I sometimes have to them.

Feeling grateful that morning flew wide the door for serenity to sweep from my heart into a sense of wholeness and well being, and I was amazed to see beauty instead of neglect.

It is with similar amazement that I consider how grateful I feel for my mother's death. This gratitude, installed by grace, has softened my heart. I feel softer, both towards losing her and losing others. This is not anything like forcing myself to feel good. That's not gratitude's style. The thing I might do to pretend or white knuckle through change is not gratitude. Neither putting on a happy face, nor rationalizing someone is in a better place, nor avoiding the hard work of grieving, nor pretending I don't miss someone will hold a candle to the brightness and warmth of gratitude. Now and again, I have tried all of those things, and worse yet, others have annoyed me with suggesting them, an unfortunate common experience. That is, until I discovered, or rediscovered, the superior mindset and freedom true gratitude brings.

It's like learning to dance or play ball. It takes a little instruction initially, some practice, and tapping into the rythm the skill requires. Once learned, you won't forget it; you won't want to forget it.

Intellectually, I know of the value of gratitude. This can help me to process what might be happening if for some reason the call of the cardinal or the orange sun's rays don't ring my gratitude bell. Why not? Do I have a low battery or something burned out? Not enough sleep? Am I eating well?

If I am not taking care of my everyday needs, I know I will run low on ports for docking gratitude. I accomodate this information about myself by purposely waking up as slowly as possible each morning, so to give gratitude a foothold if it's coming. Sometimes a piano CD a friend made trickles daintily from another room as an alarm if I must set one. Often a window is open a crack. The morning sounds may synchronize, and provide an enriched natural setting for contemplation of the abundance I sense residing in Nature and resonating within me. It is my blueprint for finding gratitude. I invite you to create as full a setting for the possibility of gratitude coming to you, as your time, energy, and money will permit, *without being zealous or adamant about the results you may or may not have.*

No stronger damper to the successful access of this blueprint is righteous expectation about the results of feeling grateful. Planning results kills the process. This limits what either you or I can do from here. I have shared my experience, but I cannot teach you to seek gratitude. I have invited you to the clear pool for a long drink, that does usually quench our thirst for peace, relief, and freedom from worry. One learns to wait with timing, as if moving into an already swinging jump rope. Play, hum, clap your hands. Send guilt, cynicism, despair and fear romping to other fields. Read (and write) poetry if it helps. Dig in the dirt. In other words, oil the hinge.

Not only will gratitude find its way to you again, it can come on a habit. Create the habit of inviting it. A secret that our Spirit never seems to forget is that the heart and the head enjoy an open door between them.

What if this door between heart and head has been slammed shut? What if even going near this door brings anxiety and fear? What if gratitude is unwanted for now? What if you believe that you need to feel the dark side of your existence, and that a lighter heart would feel false in some way to what you believe you feel today? Okay, okay, and okay respectively...and respectfully. Remember, I was the angry one for years; I was the one who attended Bible studies only if we didn't talk about God; I was the one who showed up for my mother's death, thirty-five years after my father's, gratefully, in the nick of time.

Hope

It is an amazing thought that hope is often connected to something we hear. People pay me to listen to them, and yet they are surprised when a) I hear what they believe they said, b) I hear something they didn't know they said, c) I hear what they meant to say, d) I hear what they didn't mean to say, or e) I heard more than one meaning to what they said. The process is enlightening when free from judgment, but when eclipsed by judgment, options fall away.

"Mrs. Smith, you have cancer" can be words that come with preconceived notions, or expectations connected to our worst fears. Our fears can drive hope into the wilderness to live alone, or on an isolated island. We can guess where Tom Hanks put his hope, in the movie, *Castaway,* where he plays the role of a solitary survivor, stranded on an island after his plane crashes. He appears to personify his hope in "Mr. Wilson," a volleyball. With a face drawn by his own blood, the volleyball mirrored his own hope and courage, a person stranded (metaphorically, no arms or legs), but still a presence. His hope became his only companion. In the movie, when the volleyball is lost, our hero appears to lie down to die. It is hard to find anything more lethal than lost hope.

As weavers of our lives, what colors of hope do you weave? Is hope the sweet pink threads of a rose? Is it copper, dark, and musty like the inside of a great, old cathedral? Is it the royal, deep purple, cobalt, or red of the sky in its varied designs of grandeur? Is your hope fragile, pale, and delicate? Is it young and vulnerable the way a child feels near a grandparent's authority? Is your hope filled with tradition and memorized scriptures that give it structure and form? Is your hope barely existing or gloriously alive? Is your hope silent but sweet as the vanilla scented candle? Is your hope hiding behind humor? Does your hope fill up with creativity and spill out onto a colorful canvas? Does your hope sit patiently and wait for you to return to a quiet place in your home? Is your hope willing to stretch, to learn to grow, and to find new meaning in reading and sharing?

Let those who can hope do things with a lightness of heart so that others who have less hope will benefit as well. Hope for hope. Pray for it, and for the blessing of sharing it with others.

This is my best attempt at my truth. Historically, I have sometimes used the excuse that my circumstances have differed from everyone else I have known. Literally, that may be true, but there are great similarities between us, if you too are wounded. Some basics of healing are universal. Instead of seeking someone like me, I might have taken hope from the community of those who needed to heal. I've been stubborn, hard-headed, arrogant, rude, and well hidden. At two, Mom reports I said, "I do'd it myself." Doing this project myself, whether out of habit or character flaw, leaves only me to blame for imperfections.

Gratefully, we are all imperfect, so despite more I might say, I am ending my story here, with hope that you will share your stories to each other. I encourage you to grieve, not because it isn't painful -- it is -- but because it will free you for a richer, more intimate life.

I wanted this small book to provide intimate insights for persons who knew Mom, or persons losing their own mothers. I hope to lessen your fear of death, of loss, and of the grieving process. I hope this helps you to feel less alone in your loss, as writing this has helped me to feel less alone in mine.

After returning home from Mom's death, my beautiful memories splashed onto the paper. I cried words instead of tears. Months later, in revising it, the tears came. I have vividly remembered my life, and the remembering has brought both grief and more freedom from pain.

This is enough to honor my mother, my family, and the living we unfolded together, and the dying experience she led me to know more intimately. I am grateful, and this is the note to end on, since gratitude is a doorway to hope. I will let hope be the whisper on the wind, God's breath, God's Spirit, one with yours and my sigh when we leave this life, wishing you too fondly, "Bye-Bye." *kAh*

Appendices:

Appendix A: Loss Time Line Guidelines

Appendix B: Living with Less Worry and Fear

Appendix C: Guidelines for Finding a Therapist

Appendix D: References

Appendix A : Loss Time Line Guidelines

Have a long role of butcher paper or brown paper that you can spread out while working on this, and then role up when not working on it. Take your time creating this Line.

Outline a chronology of your life, beginning with your birth and coming forward to the present. Literally, draw a long line, to create a sense of time. First, note important dates. Then list places you lived, homes you lived in, and major events. As you work, fill in with mostly facts, and secondary events and changes.

Eventually, create more detail, especially with events that stand out in your mind, **even if you do not consider them significant**. If you remembered them, they are probably more important than you realize right now.

Consider primary losses. Later, consider secondary and tertiary losses. (These are the ripples of grief coming off primary losses.) Consider losses of safety, innocence, hope, friendships, security, community, trust, knowledge, support, skills, etc.

To help you to fill in your Loss Time Line, provide answers to the following questions. Writing out your answers may help you find emotionally related losses.

What are some losses you have experienced in the recent 6-12 months? What is the most difficult loss you ever experienced? What is the earliest loss you remember? At what age did you first learn of death? What was the reaction to this loss, of others around you?

Are you open about your losses? If not, when did you shut down? At some point in time did you stop being curious about death? When, if ever, did you become fearful of dying? What historic losses did you experience? (assasinations of leaders, for example)

What losses other than deaths have you experienced? Have you moved many times? Did you grow up without brothers and sisters? Did you have grandparents?

What dreams have not happened? How do your goals in life differ now from ten years ago? Are there family members who died, cousins, aunts, and uncles? What role has death played in conversations in your family? What losses related to being "normal" have you experienced?

What relationships have you lost? How has secrecy played into your losses? How would you describe losses related to your sense of innocence? What absence in your life represents loss? What exceptionality in your life represents loss? Did you ever win one thing, and lose something else at the same time?

Share your Loss Time Line with a good listener -- someone with "ears to hear and eyes to see," to help you in the turning to heal. Have a number of people who are safe and available, so at least one will be there when you need.

Appendix B : Living with Less Worry and Fear

What kinds of things worry you the most? Is it the announcement of terminal illness, with its inevitable suffering, for you or a loved one? Or is it that you fear you will never have what you truly want out of life? This would be an experience of a loss in limbo.

When the phone rings, do you fear hearing one more terrible thing has happened in your life? Is it nearly impossible to appreciate today because of the weight of the past losses?

Do fantasies of death come in the form of nightmares? Do you often imagine funerals, hospitals, wrecks, or accidents that result in pain or death? Do you envision responses to your own or loved ones deaths?

Consider the following 12 guidelines toward ridding yourself of worry and fear. If you have tried most of them already, and found little success at doing these, it may be time to find a professional to help you move through some of your difficulties. There is no shame in needing help. Take this list with you to your session with your therapist or psychologist, noting what you have tried from the following list, and why you think this didn't work for you. Doing this will probably save you some time and money in the long run.

Using the following scale, rate yourself on each of the 12 actions to be taken toward dealing with fear and worry. This is only one measurement, but it may indicate whether or not other testing is needed.

5 = I obsess about this topic, mostly keeping to myself.
4 = I have worried that I need to deal with this topic.
3 = I repeatedly discuss this with my friends & support.
2 = I am currently in therapy about this topic.
1 = Either by myself, or with the help of a professional, I am able to use this tool to overcome fear and worry.

1. I am able to keep negative thoughts to a minimum, instead of moving into obsessing about the worst case scenarios.
2. I search for the real fear I have beneath my imaginings.
3. I have re-experienced a partial image of a trauma. I am doing the grief work connected to this old trauma.
  (I understand this may be my internal invitation toward freedom from re-victimizations; I feel I am trying to heal.)
4. I am working to replace old, outdated coping strategies.
5. I do not project what has happened to me into fears for others.
6. I am realistic about what I can and cannot do to prevent things from happening to the people I love.
7. Many times a day, I pray the Serenity Prayer, asking God for "the serenity to accept the things I cannot change, for courage to change the things I can, and for wisdom to know the difference" (This famous prayer by Reinhold Niebuhr can be found by searching "serenity prayer" on the Internet.)
8. I use my compassion in constructive ways. **I ask** what I can do to help, and specifically follow through to a conclusion.
9. If someone says I cannot help, I allow them the courtesy of leaving them alone.
10. I understand that I am a work in progress, and that making mistakes now and then is part of my growth.

11. I talk with others in ways that don't drag them into my pool of fear and worry.

12. I accept the reality that I have a lot of energy that has gone into worrying, and instead, I have learned to sing a song, write a poem, or find a way to be creative with my energy.

If you scored 12, congratulations; you truly understand the process of dealing with your fears. You are on your way to healthy. A score of 12-20 is probably a good indication that you are working toward personal freedom and serenity. A score of 20-30 indicates you may have a strong support system, but still might want to pull a professional in to discuss some of your less effective coping strategies. Also, you may be wearing at times on your friendships.

The higher the number, the more you are identifying that you worry, but without the input of professional help, or a solid network of support. While this is only one indicator, a score of 40 and above means you would probably benefit in talking with a professional who could lend some guidance, stronger than your own coping mechanisms are currently handling.

Appendix C : Guidelines for Finding a Therapist

Healing comes many ways, nearly always with dignity, honor, respect, and shame-free guidance. Healing is the business of you and God, the rest of us are only midwives. While I am honored when I am asked to participate in the process, I can't make people change -- for better or for worse.

A helper will:

1. have respectable, that is acceptable, credentials.
2. be licensed or at least accountable to a larger body of knowledge and wisdom than themselves.
3. have an understanding of how they help people (know what they know).
4. have an understanding of their limitations.
5. continue to improve and to learn.
6. be open, safe, and not condemning of beliefs unlike their own.
7. be discerning, but without taking ownership for another person's problems.
8. be nurturing.
9. have appropriate boundaries.
10. understand they are capable of making mistakes.
11. know how to apologize, and to make referrals to a more suitable helper as needed.
12. practice what they preach.

I suggest finding someone who thinks they have a great therapist, and find out why. Ask why and how this person believes he or she succeeded under the guidance of their therapist. Referrals can be a good resource.

In a brief phone interview with a recommended therapist, ask questions that will help to assure you that this counselor is appropriate for helping you do your grief work. The above criteria should be in place as best as you can discern from a phone call or perhaps a visit to their website.

Ask about their credentials and scope of practice. To whom are they accountable? Asking a therapist about their principles may be more telling than whether or not they have the same religion you do. Perhaps you made a list of your principles (after reading Chapter 7) that you could compare with the therapist's response to questions about their own principles.

Seek a counselor who is specifically familiar and competent in the area of doing grief work. How do they suggest assessing the need to grieve? Do they mention a Loss Time Line? What is their experience working with persons in grief? Ask about the professional associations to which they belong. Give the therapist an idea of your needs, so they may respond directly to that need.

When you call, you may also ask about financial arrangements, for how long appointments are scheduled, and the location of their office. For reasons of confidentiality, the therapist cannot say anything about the person who referred you, unless they explicitly have written permission to do so.

In all states, it is the law to report suspected child abuse. A professional knows how to handle this with discretion, but it does need to be reported. ALWAYS a therapist should maintain a non-sexual relationship with you, the client. If not, he or she should be reported to the Board or authorities to whom they are responsible.

If the therapist is licensed by the state you live in, you can probably look them up online, to see if they are in good standing. Shame-free sense of humor, ease of talking, sincerity, and openness are usually good signs. Having poor boundaries is not a good sign. There is usually no obligation to come back if you do not feel comfortable with the room, the atmosphere, the information, or your introductory session.

Not every therapist is a match to every patient. What

is important is that the therapist finds ways to help you to feel comfortable with the process, even if you are feeling pain. At any time, your therapist should be all right to refer you elsewhere if you ask, without any malice or bad feelings toward you.

Plan to do some transference on your therapist. They should be professional enough to recognize this phenomenon when it happens, even though you probably won't. Transference is the process of putting someone else's face upon your therapist's face. He or she should be able to help you to see what you are doing, but unfortunately, therapists sometimes do counter-transference. For example, you see your alcoholic dad in your therapist, and he sees you back as the rebellious son he had. This therapy won't do well, until the transference/counter transference is cleared up. (Meaning, he's not your dad, and you aren't his son.) Therapy can be a tremendously freeing process, when done well. Keep searching for someone right for you.

A therapist/client relationship may be long-term, such as the relationship you have with your physician, but this relationship is best defined by dependency being replaced by interdependency over the years. In time, this relationship may become valued for its wisdom and support, and from a place of adult to adult interaction, rather than a relationship with a strong power difference. If you are still feeling needy or nervous about receiving the approval of your therapist a few years into the relationship, you may want to look at the level of codependency that may have developed.

Counselors are also not above having their own issues. Look at how many of my own I have acknowledged in this book. Helpers often come from difficult and complicated histories, which complements our compassion at the same time as creating our individual Achilles' heels. Expectations of perfection probably end more therapeutic relationships than any one other factor (from both sides.) If you think your therapist is no longer helping you, you might be doing both of you a good turn to admit this to him or her. This is another opportunity to express your voice, to grow, and to grieve, of course.

In your search for therapy, it may help to know the general hierarchy among licensed and degreed individuals giving counsel. The top rung (and most expensive) is represented by Psychiatrists (Medical Doctors with a specialization in Psychiatry) who are the main source for prescribing medication, and the authorities for working with the truly mentally ill. Secondly, psychologists usually have PhD's and some specialty. In many states Licensed Social Workers are third highest, but not usually licensed to prescribe medication. Insurance coverage is usually available for these top three, but be aware that a diagnosis may also be needed to receive this coverage There is still some stigma to receiving a mental diagnosis (unfortunately) in our country.

Three more licensures are available in most states. Licensed Professional Counselor, Licensed Marriage and Family Therapist, and Licensed Acohol and Drugs of Abuse Counselor. Each has a National organization that helps to define both ethical standards and scope of practice. Certified counselors, including most bereavement counselors, are reputable, but not governed by a State Board. EAP assistance is available through some companies. At least a Master's level degree is usually needed for these kinds of professions.

Appendix D: References

The best resource for you is your own ability to inquire. Inquire within and without.

Introduction:

1. Madeleine L'Engle, *The Rock That is Higher: Story as Truth* (Colorado Springs, CO.: WaterBrook Press, 2002

Chapter 1:

2. Active Parenting USA Headquarters, 1955 Vaughn Rd. N.W. Suite 108, Kennesaw, GA. 30144-7808 www.activeparenting.com PH: 800-825-0060 or 800-235-7755, Fax: 770-429-0334

3. Tom Hickman, *Death, A User's Guide* (Delta Trade Paperback Ed. NY, 2003)

Chapter 4:

4. Thomas Lewis, M.D., Fari Amini, M.D., and Richard Lannon, M.D., *A General Theory of Love* (Random House, New York, 2000 - Vintage Edition, 2001).

Chapter 5:

5. www.codependents.org (Codependency Anonymous)

6. www.al-anon.alateen.org (Al -Anon Resource)

7. www.alcoholics-anonymous.org (12 Step Resource)

Chapter 7: Meditations read to Mother, taken from:

8. Billy Graham, *Hope for Each Day; Words of Wisdom and Faith* (Thomas Nelson, TN, 2002)

Chapter 8:

9. Windows by Active Parenting, (see Reference in Chtr 1)

10. www.legalzoom.com

11. www.PrePaidLegal.com

12. www.1StopLegal.com

13. Caring Resources in Nashville, TN. The publication is titled: ***Help! Where Are All My Papers? A practical guide to identify and organize "must know" information.*** www. caringresources.com

14. *Long-Term Care; Your Financial Planning Guide* by Phyllis Shelton (Kensington Books, 2003).

15. Bonell Good Samaritan Center, 708 22nd St., P.O. Box 1508, Greeley, CO. 80632-1508 PH: (970) 352-6082 www. good-sam.com

Chapter 11:

16. The Holy Bible RSV (Thomas Nelson & Sons, NY, 1953) (Acts 28:27)

Sampling on Patience, (p. 150)

17. Oswald Chambers, *My Utmost for His Highest, p. 123* (Uhrichsville OH.: Barbour & Co., Inc., 1963)

Chapter 12:

18. The Holy Bible RSV (Mk 10:13-16 RSV) (Luke 18:15-17 RSV) (Mt 19:14 RSV)

Part II:

19. Ed. Jeffrey A. West, M.D., *The Complete Medical Guide for the Family Caregiver,* (LifeLine Press, Washington, D.C.)

20. Robert Bornstein and Mary Languirand, *When Someone You Love Needs Nursing Home, Assisted Living, or In-Home Care,* (New Market Press, New York, 2002)

21. WholeCare Connections, Inc, here in Nashville, TN was founded by Elizabeth Moss. www.WholeCareConnections. com Fax: 615-298-9202; Phone: 615-298-9201

2000 Warfield Dr. Nashville, TN 37215

22. See #13.

23. See #14.

PART II

Encouragement for Caregivers

Decisions about caregiving are of the utmost importance for the welfare and well-being of every friend or family member involved. The worst thing you can do is to plan nothing. Nearly all caregiving advice says "planning is power." Avoiding the hard questions won't make any problem (if there is one) go away, and many problems become more complicated when left unattended. Learn to ask questions -- even ones you think are dumb.

The sooner you understand your need for support, which will include professional guidance sooner or later, the better you will digest the life-altering transition you've entered. You can begin with helpful books. For example, if medical questions are pushing to the forefront, visit your local library to view *the Complete Medical Guide for the Family Caregiver,* Edited by Jeffrey A. West, M.D., published by LifeLine Press, Washington, D.C.

Medical topics can come with such frustrations as words we don't know, conditions we can't understand, and consequences beyond our control. The good news is, the medical world believes they have good answers, whether or not you fully understand them. The bad news is, sometimes you must ask the right questions to get the answers the medical world believes they have. Good communication is paramount, and a responsibility that will fall to the caregiver if the care receiver is using up their energy being sick. The fearful prediction is that everyone will run out of steam before the train gets to the station.

When Someone You Love Needs Nursing Home, Assisted Living, or In-Home Care, by Robert Bornstein and Mary Languirand is a book that gives exemplary advice about the topics listed in the title. It is a 2002 publication from New Market Press, New York. This book can start you on the road to asking the needed questions of both the care recipient, and the professionals with whom you must dialogue.

Bornstein and Languirand warn us, "the more complex the problem, the more highly trained the caregiver must be and the higher the cost" (p. 32). If you begin caregiving because there is "no other option," "it was the next right thing to do," or "it's just Mom (or Dad) moving in with us," the questions still need to be asked and answered. It's okay to begin asking questions slowly and carefully, so as to reduce the level of alarm and friction, but it's not okay to ignore the needs of the care receiver, the care giver, and other family members, especially those involved in the living situation. If someone begins paying a price they resent, increase the process of safe dialogue-- not out of demand or entitlement, but out of wise compassion for everyone involved.

Grief will be the emotion that warns you quickest of an imbalance in meeting the needs of family members. If you have read Part I of this book, you know that grief seldom announces itself as "grief." It will more likely come with friction, aggitation, confusion, alarm, anger, sadness, or fear.

When changes happen quickly, so do the losses, along with a flood of emotions.

It won't be easy to continue with your daily routines, meet new challenges of caregiving, grieve your losses, and remember to ask the right questions. If you *can* develop some skills of grieving along the way, congratulations!

Ask yourself these questions if you are still wondering whether or not caregiving has actually arrived.

Did you ignore the concerns of (your version of) Aunt Claire who hadn't seen your mother in six months? Listen to the warnings of those who have not familiarized themselves yet with changes in your loved one. Are you and other family members rationalizing with such phrases as "that's just what happens to all older folks" and "she's doing a lot better than her neighbor"? It is unfair to your loved one to compare her to anyone else.

Are you making things up in your head because you don't want to take the time to discuss your Dad's use of the car? Are you intimidated by their angry responses when you bring up the topics related to your elderly parent's future?

Are you ignoring your "gut's" concern? Are you condemning your fears as irrational, or justifying your avoidance? Are you allowing status quo, your finances, your promotion at work, the activities of the children to keep you too busy to really look at the needs of someone who is important to you? Who is depending upon you to care for them when they cannot care for themselves? Have you allowed only partial changes where stronger actions need to be taken?

If your answer is "Yes" to even a few questions, begin studying right away. Go to the library or buy some books.

Start making local phone calls. Become knowledgable. Get some help.

What if you have clearly assumed a caretaking role in nearly every way mentioned above, but you still have not sought professional guidance?

When will your care receiver need to have a mental or psychological evaluation? When will they need an assessment of their physical skills? Is your doctor available to assist someway in this process? When and how is a pastor or lay minister helpful? Have medical tests been run to rule out diseases? Have you researched therapy for the family system that will be affected as a whole unit?

I am inviting you to think directionally. Think about the journey. Think in terms of growth and development, not a final product. Think in terms of the next right thing to do. Break this overwhelming task into small do-able steps.

I suggest a step-wise process (See Figure A) through the maze of caregiving. The following steps naturally progress from one to the other, and are repeated many times throughout the developmental changes of life. These are the steps of the life-death dance, all along the journey. They are as predictable as a dip, and a swing, a step and a turn of a ballroom dance. Being comfortable with each step as part of the whole will help you to identify where you are today.

Two people are seldom (if ever) in exactly the same spot on any given topic. It makes us feel more comfortable to believe we are, but our life experiences are both unique and shared at any given moment. What you are experiencing is not exactly what your loved one is experiencing. As much as you are able, you both will need to learn to relate to and

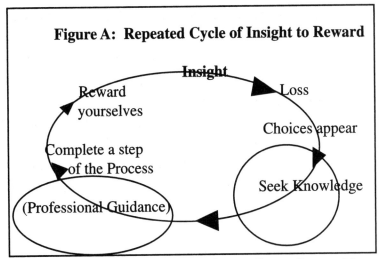

Figure A: Repeated Cycle of Insight to Reward

empathize with each other's experience. Generally speaking, the ballroom is full of dancers dancing to different tunes.

A healthy teenager, for example, experiences awakenings, **insights**, that are very different than the elderly experiencing awakening into their final phase of life. Regardless of age, however, every awakening is followed by a sense of more or less **loss** for the way things were (second-choice grief, p.29) New **choices**, including responsibilities and obligations, follow. Lessons come from training, books, professional advice, friends and other family members, bringing **knowledge** for a more complete understanding. Then there is the action of the new **process**, including each accomplishment, small or otherwise. **Reward** happens when the team's efforts are realized as success.

1) **Insight**
2) **Loss**
3) **Choices**
4) **Knowledge**
5) **Process**
6) **Reward.**

Insight - Insight may happen quickly or over time. If the insight feels like you're being poked repeatedly in the same spot, the location of this insight may feel bruised by now. If your loved one repeatedly gets angry whenever you attempt to discuss their need for some assistance, they are probably ahead of you, well into feeling their losses. Moving on to doing some grief work together may open up the communication system toward change. The first action will be to grieve. If your insight regards a change in a medical condition, there will still be losses with which to contend, but the choices will be different. In either case, one doesn't stay long at insight. One moves quickly into realizing the accompanying loss or losses.

Loss - If you have been reading *Grief Work, Grief in Limbo*, or working on your *Loss Time Line* in relation to Part I of this book, you will be understanding the interference grief can present in your daily living. Loss can produce a mental fog, difficulty in concentration, loss of appetite, and waves of sadness, to name a few symptoms. Depression is distinguished from grieving because it is more likely to hang around like a continual dark cloud over us than to come and go in waves of emotion, as grief does.

Both grief and depression can affect the brain chemistry. Complicated grieving sometimes requires short-term anti-depressant medication (see your doctor for this.) *Chronic* depression may require anti-depressant medication indefinitely. Loss doesn't automatically throw us into a clinical depression, but we can certainly feel "down" or "overwhelmed." The grieving process includes the insight of discovering our truth. Then, the work of grief is to share that truth with someone safe and non-judging of your insights. This provides a witness and hopefully a supportive person along the journey. Doing the next right thing moves us from feeling the pain in a helpless way, to feeling we have some choices we can make. Part I extensively details this summary.

Choice - It is wise to dialogue with others in the process of making choices within caregiving. Unilateral decisions may feel controling, uncooperative, uncaring, bossy, disrespectful, or resistent, depending upon which "side" you are on. If someone's life is in immediate and absolute danger, then a decision may need to be made quickly, and the consequences dealt with later. We grab a child out of harms way, and "discuss" it later. With an aging parent or disabled family member, discussion of choices is an empowered part of the planning.

When I went to talk with mother about my sibling's insights into a serious decrease in her ability to continue driving, I did go with the idea of asking her to stop. I did not begin with that idea as a request. I simply went to her to talk about her insights into her driving. We quickly moved to the losses she had already been experiencing.

"Well, you know I haven't driven at night for some time now. That's not safe," she said.

"Are you still feeling safe when you drive during the day?" "Oh, I think so," she said hesitantly.

"You aren't sure about your safety during the day?"

"No, one day, I wasn't certain which side of the road I was on." Right here I worked hard to avoid being dramatic or squeal in terror, "You're kidding, I hope!" Instead, I think

I said something like "Really?"

"Well, the sun was in my eyes as I turned the corner, and it was a double lane that went into one lane each way -- over by the college..."

By now, I am envisioning the worst possible scenario, ending with mother having a head on collision with someone. I pulled myself back out of the pitfall of worry, which as you remember is inefficient compassion, and asked, "When do you think it will be time to quit driving during the day?"

"Oh, I don't know really."

"Mom, you've had a really good driving record. Very few accidents. Would you rather stop on top of your driving, or wait until you have to because you hit someone, or helped to create an accident where someone hurts you?"

"Well, of course I would rather quit before something bad happens."

I let her think about this for awhile. Mother, liking her "sensible person" reputation didn't take long to come around to the part of the discussion. "What would I do with my car? Does anyone in the family need or want it?"

This is a big choice -- a big step down for an elderly person who has enjoyed their independence in their transportation. Every decision should honor the length and depth of discussion needed, so that the air is cleared of concern, honorably filled with truth about the losses, and given time to attend the secondary losses that ripple off the primary loss. Close attention to the care receiver's true physical and mental abilities should be used with dignity and kindness, not threats or accusations. It is okay to share in the sadness that your loved one feels before moving into a choice upon which you both agree.

Knowledge - Developing a "passion for patience" (page 149) is essential here. Don't skimp on finding more information that will help in the decision making process. Procrastination doesn't help, period. Wasting time just thinking about researching something won't find those alternatives. Action is part of finding more knowledge to support doing the next right thing. If your loved one has the skills (and many elderly do), let them find some new evidence on the Internet, or from any number of the resources mentioned in this book. If your care recipient appears to have lost heart, care giving has probably reached a level of seeking wise and professional help in order to restore the action of mutually working together within well-informed choices.

The Process needs to work for both of you, and all persons involved in your lives together. No one should feel sacrificed if there is any way to possibly avoid it. Knowledge-based caring provides more choices. Seek guidance. Seek wisdom. Learn from the mistakes others have made before you.

Then, take time to celebrate The Reward of accomplishing every step that you make, no matter how small. Without taking "reward time" the cycle will feel endless. Celebrate the completion of the circle. Yes, another loss will show up to process. Taking time to celebrate will add strength and confidence toward handling the next challenge. Rewards should be chosen wisely, and from the place of health whenever possible. Obviously, rewarding the care receiver with a cigarette, when they are dying of lung cancer, and struggle with emphysema might not be the best choice. Try not to link medicines and drugs that relieve pain with "rewards."

Celebrate success with time, energy, and intimacy when it is possible. These are the things dying people often miss the most. Play a game of checkers, listen to some music together, take a drive, listen to books on tape with them.

The Reward is about "good for us, we have been able to communicate and resolve a difficult decision." It is not about getting one more thing "out of the way." It is about the serenity and satisfaction we feel when we work together to create a solution.

Diffficult Decisions

How can I find a trustworthy caregiver? I have sought help from a care giver agency in Nashville for help with this difficult question. WholeCare Connections, Inc, here in Nashville, TN was founded by Elizabeth Moss, a highly qualified professional caregiver. She suggests the following questions to ask when you need to hire a private care service. While there are probably no absolutely right answers, I have put in parentheses possible answers to help guide your understanding.

1. May I contact others who have used your service? (They should have a list of references.)
2. What is your philosophy of care/what is your mission statement? (The mission statement of WholeCare Connection is *to care for the whole person through connecting the needs of Seniors with caring professionals.*)
3. What type of family caregiver support do you offer? (Ongoing training seminars would be good.)

4. Why should I use you over another agency (They may not know what other agencies do, but use an agency who does criminal background screens and who checks the national abuse registry. Your agency should be willing to share many support resources, both Internet and local organizations.)

5. What kind of plan do you present or help us to create? (They should have a way to present a clear plan of care, and how they will communicate and modify those plans as care needs change.)

6. What happens in the event a caregiver is ill or doesn't show up for work? (Look for depth of coverage; you may see up to 5 caregivers in the situation of a 24 hour/7 day week.)

7. Does the same caregiver come each time? (Possibly not -- the hours may make a difference.)

8. What will a caregiver look like, who is a "good fit" for my loved one? (A "good fit" is a caregiver who allows the patient as much control and dignity as possible -- not a person who does everything for a patient, but someone who interacts well with the family, and understands the learning and loss curves involved in this transitional dynamic.)

9. What do you look for in an employee? (Their credentials and criteria should come close to your expectations. Remember, you have done some reading!)

10. How long is the probation or adjustment period expected? (One week is usually adequate.)

11. How do you bill? (This coincides with the clearly outlined Care Management Plan.)

12. Will I be required to sign a contract? (You may need to agree to hire this caregiver service only, or agree to the caregiver using your automobile, or waive liability. If the contract looks scary or rather exacting, you might want an

attorney to take a look at it.)

13. Do you have workman's compensation benefits and liability insurance. (Yes, and Yes. See #12)

14. What does the certification of your caregivers cover? (Credentials make a difference regarding the administration of medication, and certain kinds of treatments. Know what your caregiver is qualified to do and what he or she is not qualified to do *ahead* of hiring them. All professionals have a "scope of practice." It simply outlines these areas they can and cannot do.)

What's okay to look for in a caregiver?

Elizabeth Moss tells me that a professional appearance is important, and provides clues about a person's attitudes and professionalism, but suggests looking beyond generational norms (i.e. blue hair), racial or religious biases or requirements about the caregiver being a certain size. They do need to have the health and capacity to perform their job duties. A good caregiver is observant, and instinctively aware of the care recipient's needs, including those needs to retain as much independence as possible. They communicate well (and sometimes more loudly or slowly than you may be used to hearing.) They are not arrogant, but instead self-confident. You need to feel "in good hands."

Additionally, Elizabeth Moss tells me that a good caregiver must be able to be tolerant and accepting of ideas and beliefs that may not be their own; care receivers are often different from their caregivers in age, gender, ethnicity and beliefs. Caregivers must understand that care receivers are experiencing "the unknown." A caregiver may have "seen this a hundred times," but the care receiver has only lived it once.

The care receiver is experiencing new losses, daily sometimes. It is not to be taken personally by the caregiver. If you are a family member providing the caregiving, you may be into the unknown as well. This may be the biggest reason to include some level of professional help -- so that not everyone is new to the situation. Your open-mindedness is a huge asset during these difficult transitions.

Creative problem solving is often best attained by minds in harmony and community with each other. Balance passion with even temperment and sense of humor with dignified and deep concern. Balance getting things done with patience for the eleventh hour some things take to happen. Find a wellspring of sustenance from your own continued healing, and your faith and hope in God.

Long-distance Help

Again, stay focused on the process. Long-distance relatives are receiving the information in echo format. They will go through the same steps, but often one or two steps behind you. This compounds your own sense of loss of someone being there beside you. It is easy to mistake their dance as resistant, as opposed to simply a step behind. Keep others informed with not only the agreed upon next right thing you and the care receiver have decided upon, but also the thought process you took getting to that decision. They cannot be expected to understand that you are going to Kalamazoo instead of Panama City until they realize a summer storm is expected in Panama City.

Share what you read and what you know in some of the same small bites you chewed, via phone calls or emails. Again, try not to take ignorance as negativity or resistance. Everyone grieves differently, and everyone copes with their pain differently. Not everyone copes in healthy ways. Remember the ballroom filled with different dancers, and try to practice acceptance and compassionate understanding. You may need extra support from sources other than your family members.

Share the Cycle of Insight to Reward (page 192), and include where you are on the circle. This may help each of you to find ways to deal with the inevitable delayed emotional responses, even if you are instant messaging.

Allow for long-distance responses to be part of the planning process. Keeping the family in step with the care receiver may be one of the most caring gifts you can give.

Note:

If you find yourself hiring and firing more than two specially chosen teams, back up to get some individual, and/or some family therapy. Either you are experiencing multiple losses (a doctor dies or retires; a caregiver has to quit for personal reasons) while you are trying to deal with your own losses, or your discernment of yours and your loved one's needs isn't exactly accurate.

Either way, it may be time to expand the team. Life is full of complications, getting therapy does not reflect failure, but rather a need for a wider perspective than what you can currently see.

Unfortunately professionals are often asked to "fix" something past the time they were originally needed, partly because you may not recognize the symptoms of certain kinds of problems. Even if you do see the signs, you may not know what it will take to turn things around. Many people are accustomed to ignoring their own emotional and physical needs, and miss or ignore changes that require yet more attention. In addition, what is "familiar" seems "okay." For example, until it becomes an obvious imbalance, we don't worry too much about "an attitude adjustment," "going through a phase,"or being "just like other old folks." Wisely, we are not overly concerned about changes that are naturally part of growing up, but if you have some questions, getting a professional opinion should help you define to what extent there is a need.

Over the years I have received both some great therapy and some bad therapy. I have also experienced "non-therapy" and therapeutic experiences such as gardening, writing, traveling, etc. Healing has certain requirements, just like a plant needs the right light, water, and soil to grow. We too have "growing conditions." We need safety, harmony, nurturing, and faith, for starters.

Sometimes, it is hard for people to see the necessary "growth" going into the final stage of living, but being able to see potential in the stage of dying is quintessential to receiving the gifts that come with this stage. One of the most endearing gifts to come from a loved one's dying is that of healing. Broken dreams and burdened hearts may need more healing, even than their bones and organs.

Being attuned to the ultimate need of a care receiver requires intimately listening to their grieving. Making it possible for a care receiver to grieve, before they shut down completely is a profound gift to the care receiver. Of course, they often will be unskilled in the process of grieving. Explore their areas of loss, by reading together different chapters from Part I.

The continued unfolding of losses can give care receivers a sense of loss of independence, directionality, purpose, and worthiness in their lives, so it is important to deal with these from both sides -- what they have given, and what they now receive.

The following indicators of change will need to be addressed as they arrive. Loss of motive, and loss of interest can be signs of either grief or depression. Provide someone who can witness to your loved one's shared truth. (See *Grief Work,* p. 48)

When a friend dies, follow up with maintaining connections with others who share this loss. Find a symbol of this special friendship, do the grief work, and talk about the absence of this special person.

Watch for medical losses, such as eyesight, memory, motor skills, and fine skills. Get assessments as needed. Look for activities, physical therapists, and specialists to help with retaining as many skills as possible, even when driving and transportability suffer.

If the community is in constant flux, find one or two stable members to build memories around. There is nothing like intimate connections to revive our sense of worthiness. It is best when an adult makes this connection; it is too much to ask a teenager to become a "stable relationship" for a dying grandparent, for example. Let the children come, and bring their spontaneous beauty, and freely leave when they choose.

When the care receiver can no longer keep up with the

bills or the mail, nor with the changes in others, acknowledge this loss of independency and perception. Rather than take over completely, see if there is a way to find time to pay the bills together, or go through a newspaper, or a church bulletin together. Read to the care receiver from their favorite way to stay informed. This will create several positive layers of gratitude that opens wide the door between heart and head.

Of course, they have slowed down, but don't we all need to go slower at times? Find a time that works for you, in which to share "slow." Hire others to share slow, when you need to go faster than slow. Try to never send the message that you are too busy for someone you love. Filling in some spaces where you cannot go yourself, however, is not about being too busy for them, it is about creating imaginative answers at times to meet your own needs.

As the care receiver shows evidence of loss of health, allow for the grief to follow. Then allow yourself and the care receiver to adapt to their new person inside. As medical paradoxical effects arrive (see page 126), stay truthful and understand it is part of the step down situation.

Allow for the elderly to comfort you too. Give them opportunities to counsel and hear you. Bring them dignity, honor, faith, and grace, and they will hopefully bring these things to their dying.

Grief-in-limbo is a huge component of the continuing losses felt by those care givers and care receivers inside of the sometimes long and arduous transition through aging, terminal illnesses, or handicapping conditions. For your own sake, learn about grief-in-limbo (page 113). If you have enough time and energy, please try to read all of Part I, for the tools to deal with your own losses.

I have found some excellent resources for Caregivers in Nashville, Tennessee. I also know that Caregiver resources are fast becoming overwhelmed. Hopefully, it is a service area that will increase nationwide. Two excellent resources for beginning the understanding around the paperwork and the financial planning are listed below:

A great workbook published by Caring Resources in Nashville, TN. The publication is titled ***Help! Where Are All My Papers? A practical guide to identify and organize "must know" information.*** One notebook they sell has special Caregiver Information included, and a second one is without the caregiver insert. Either can be ordered through www.caringresources.com.

Long-Term Care; Your Financial Planning Guide by Phyllis Shelton (Kensington Books, 2003) covers financial planning for Long-Term Care, Medicare and Medicaid topics in particular.

Please ask for help, so that...
you continue to have the oxygen mask to your own face, you receive some of the gifts within the final phase of life, and you can arrive at a place of enough. If we can simply let each other know the preciousness of love and life in as many moments as possible, have we not given what God has given us?

Index

Author's Credentials

Ms. Kathleen Haskett has a Master's Degree in Education from the University of Northern Colorado. Her Bachelor's Degree is from Colorado State University in Music Education. She has more than 1000 hours college credits beyond her Master's Degree.

Her specialty is metacognition, the study of how we know what we know and how we learn what we learn. She is licensed by the State of Tennessee in Alcohol and Drug Counseling. She has studied and worked many years in spiritual bereavement as well. Over the past fourteen years, since moving to Nashville, she has seen people for more than 11,000 hours of counseling and education. This is her first book.